Advance Praise for
From Conflict to Conciliation:
How to Defuse Difficult Situations

By William W. Purkey, John J. Schmidt,
and John M. Novak

"From the classroom to the boardroom, it's inevitable for conflicts to happen. This book will introduce you to the Six Cs, a logical process to tame those disagreements. The liberally sprinkled real-life anecdotes will keep you reading, and better yet, learning."

—Alexis Ludewig, Adjunct Instructor

"A very important and timely book that is well grounded in conflict theory and research. I especially appreciate that the strategies go beyond merely ending the conflict, but also speak to healing and seeking reconciliation. Purkey, Schmidt, and Novak have produced another winner to help educators create inviting and joyful schools."

—Sally Butzin, President, Institute for School Innovation

"This book is a valuable, useful resource for all educators and administrators and is a significant contribution to the topic of conflict resolution."

—Diane Smith, Counselor

"The Six-C approach provides a framework within which people can work together to attack the problem, not each other. By ending each conflict with conciliation, the people who use this approach in schools, hospitals, homes, and businesses will be able to do much more than resolve conflict—they can build each other up so future conflicts will be easier to resolve."

—Bob Bowen, Chief Executive Office

"Effective problem-solving skills are essential in the home, school, community, and in business and industry. The Six-C Process provides sequential steps and practical procedures to cultivate respect and solve problems."

—Dallas J. Blankenship, Senior Consultant

"When your office door bursts open with an angry parent, teacher, or child, combat has already commenced and it is too late to regret your decision to not purchase this book beforehand."

—Billy Tate, Principal

"The Six Cs provide strategies to support us to move from conflict to conciliation in a most effective and economical manner. They also open up a new way of thinking to turn potential conflicts into possible means for mutual growth through this meaningful and inviting process."

—Peter Kai-Hung Wong, Chief Curriculum Development Officer

"I highly recommend this book to anyone who works with today's youth. It will decrease teasing and bullying issues. I have used the Six Cs for several years at my school and it works!"

—Tom Carr, Elementary School Counselor

"A practical guide to help educators and others who deal with the public determine how to choose your battles and deal with them at the least aggressive level using a logical and respectful process."

—James A. Ratledge, School Improvement Consultant

"An ethically sensitive and compelling perspective on dealing with inevitable life conflicts in ways that are positive, beneficial, and self- and others-enhancing."

—Betty L. Siegel, President Emeritus

"This book contains a wealth of strategies to use on a daily basis for interacting effectively with others. Educators will enjoy teaching these valuable life skills to their students and seeing the positive results."

—Jenny Edwards, Faculty, Fielding Graduate University

"Every teacher should study the Six-C Process. The authors provide a positive, constructive, and hands-on approach to dealing with challenging situations. What a great process for educators to use!"

—David A. Chapman, Superintendent

"A truly brilliant guide to help the reader assess the inevitable conflicts of daily life! Through a step-by-step process, the authors share pointed questions that can prevent conflicts of life and work from becoming overwhelming. Readers will find this useful for building personal relationships as well as professional ones."

—Sue Bowen, Retired Assistant Superintendent

"The Six-C Process adds a unique dimension to conflict resolution. My experience with the Six Cs integrated in the Grow With Guidance System produced powerful and empowering results. Thank you for this dynamic book!"

—Tommie R. Radd, Counselor

"With scenarios for reference and practice, and research supporting the steps of the Six-C Process, this book affords the educator practical examples and specific guidelines for handling challenging situations at all levels of intensity. This will be an amazing resource for teachers and administrators!"

—Lori Grossman, Manager, Academic Training
Professional Development Services

FROM CONFLICT TO Conciliation

To a lifetime of family, friends, and colleagues who
have invited us to work through conflicts and move beyond conciliation

FROM
CONFLICT
TO
Conciliation

How
to
Defuse
**DIFFICULT
SITUATIONS**

**WILLIAM W. PURKEY
JOHN J. SCHMIDT
JOHN M. NOVAK**

CORWIN
A SAGE Company

For information:

Corwin
A SAGE Company
2455 Teller Road
Thousand Oaks,
    California 91320
(800) 233-9936
Fax: (800) 417-2466
www.corwin.com

SAGE India Pvt. Ltd.
B 1/I 1 Mohan Cooperative
    Industrial Area
Mathura Road, New Delhi 110 044
India

SAGE Ltd.
1 Oliver's Yard
55 City Road
London EC1Y 1SP
United Kingdom

SAGE Asia-Pacific Pte. Ltd.
33 Pekin Street #02-01
Far East Square
Singapore 048763

Printed in the United States of America

Library of Congress Cataloging-in-Publication Data

From conflict to conciliation: how to defuse difficult situations/William Watson Purkey, John J. Schmidt, John M. Novak, editors.
    p. cm.
Includes bibliographical references.
ISBN 978-1-4129-7986-3 (pbk.)
    1. School management and organization. 2. School crisis management. 3. Conflict management. I. Purkey, William Watson. II. Schmidt, John J., 1946- III. Novak, John M. IV. Title.

LB2805.F82 2010
371.2—dc22   2009044107

This book is printed on acid-free paper.

10   11   12   13   14   10   9   8   7   6   5   4   3   2   1

Acquisitions Editor:	Jessica Allan
Editorial Assistant:	Joanna Coelho
Production Editor:	Eric Garner
Copy Editor:	Adam Dunham
Typesetter:	C&M Digitals (P) Ltd.
Proofreader:	Joyce Li
Indexer:	Wendy Allex
Cover Designer:	Michael Dubowe
Graphic Designer:	Anthony Paular

Contents

Preface

Welcome to *From Conflict to Conciliation.* This book introduces you to a straightforward, principled, and systematic process for defusing troublesome situations in a desirable and efficient manner. We have named this approach the Six-C Process, with which we identify and explain six distinct levels of functioning when handling conflicts: *concern, confer, consult, confront, combat,* and *conciliate.* In applying the six Cs, your primary strategy is to move *reluctantly* to higher levels in measured response only as each becomes necessary.

Concern is identifying latent and actionable concerns.

Confer is using nonthreatening signal systems to express a concern.

Consult is reviewing the situation collaboratively.

Confront is considering and giving clear warning of sanctions.

Combat is taking sustained action with logical consequences.

Conciliation is healing the wounds of combat.

The Six-C Process works for us and others, and we believe it will work for you.

This book is a distillation of the research, writing, and practice of three individuals with quite diverse backgrounds representing educational philosophy, educational psychology, and counselor education. The three of us believe our professional diversity gives the book a creative and practical approach to handling difficult and challenging situations at all levels of intensity.

In writing this book, we had many opportunities to put into practice what we preach. Because the three of us come from different academic disciplines, we sometimes hold strong, divergent viewpoints about the topics covered. Despite our professional diversity and varied viewpoints, we were able to collaborate in this effort and find common ground. The process we present in this book works well and served us as a navigational compass in this project. Without this gyrocompass, we never would have finished it.

The Six-C Process is a democratically oriented, perceptually anchored method of handling conflict. Although it is immediately practical, it also is a theoretical way of relating to oneself, others, and the world. We base the Six-C Process on five interlocking assumptions:

1. People involved in conflict should be treated as able, valuable, and responsible participants.

2. Conflict resolution can be viewed as a collaborative, cooperative activity.

3. The process used in addressing conflict influences the results.

4. People possess untapped potential in solving conflicts.

5. This potential can be realized by a systemic process designed to help people intentionally resolve conflicts in desired ways.

At the beginning, we want to stress that this book is not solely about resolving conflicts. While conflicts are inevitable and can be uncomfortable, dangerous, and even tragic, we believe that conflicts are part of everyday life and can be beneficial. Moreover, advocating change without generating the prospect of conflict is almost impossible.

In human relationships, creativity and innovation bring about new ways of thinking and fresh courses of action. Such newness produces the potential for tension among divergent people with incompatible ideas. This is certainly true in education and allied professions where acquiring new information and making behavioral change become primary goals.

Conflicts can offer the opportunity to enhance relationships, learn new information, alter perceptions, and create new directions. Handled within a beneficial framework that applies respectful processes, conflict can provide relatively limitless opportunity for human development. We doubt that any advances in this world have occurred without some level of conflict among the protagonists or between opposing perspectives.

Our mission in writing this book is to propose a process to help you prevent conflicts from becoming overwhelming. Finding the right level of "whelm" makes creative growth possible in challenging situations. Simply ending conflicts through decree, indifference, power plays, or other means is insufficient. Therefore, a major purpose of this book is to demonstrate how you can bring people together to mend all types of conflicts.

Because we reject the use of coercion and force as routine instruments of policy, we advocate for thoughtful, peaceful strategies to handle myriad types of conflict. This book will help you to be reasonably comfortable in life by avoiding conflict when productive alternatives are available to you.

We present this book primarily for educators and other professionals who work in schools—teachers, administrators, teachers in training, counselors, psychologists, social workers, nurses, curriculum specialists, and more. In addition, we believe the Six-C Process will be of value to a broad range of professional helpers who work with people and their concerns. The Six-C Process has potential for people in many settings across a variety of concerns and conflicts.

The Six-C Process is not a magic formula but rather a practical procedure for dealing with people in ethical and efficient ways. We believe you will find this book useful in dealing with many conflicts in your personal and professional relationships. Writing it was both enjoyable and educational, and we are delighted to share this experience with you.

Acknowledgments

The three authors would like to thank those who contributed to this book. Our wives, Imogene, Pat, and Linda, for putting up with us during the writing of this book. They can attest to the usefulness of the Six-C Process. We are grateful to colleagues that have used concepts of the process in their work. In particular, we thank Tom Carr, a counselor in North Carolina, who described how he used the Six-C Process in working with children; Jim Ratledge, a former elementary school principal in Tennessee, who shared with us how he applied concepts of the process in a terrifying hostage situation; and William Tate, a primary school principal in Belfast, Northern Ireland. William received the Member of the British Empire award from Her Majesty the Queen for his advocacy of schools and help with reconciliation of communities in Northern Ireland after 40 years of conflict. He has used the Six-C principles to obtain desirable outcomes in a most difficult situation. We thank all the researchers and writers who provided a scholarly foundation for this work. We are also indebted to Jessica G. Allan, Senior Acquisitions Editor at Corwin, for her encouragement and patience, and to the following peer reviewers who gave us excellent suggestions in producing this book:

Andrea Burke
English/Language Arts Teacher, NBCT
Kalamazoo Public Schools
Kalamazoo, MI

Dr. Cathy Galland
Curriculum Director
Republic R-III School District
Republic, MO

Lori Grossman
Manager, Academic Training, Professional Development Services
Houston Independent School District
Houston, TX

Alexis Ludewig
Adjunct Instructor
Fox Valley Technical College
Appleton, WI

Diane Smith
Counselor
Smethport Area School District
Smethport, PA

About the Authors

William W. Purkey, EdD, is *professor emeritus* of counselor education at The University of North Carolina-Greensboro and cofounder of The International Alliance for Invitational Education. A noted author, researcher, speaker, and leader, Dr. Purkey has authored nearly 100 articles and more than a dozen books.

John J. Schmidt, EdD, is *professor emeritus* of counselor education at East Carolina University where he chaired the department for 14 years. Author of more than 50 professional articles and nearly 20 books and manuals, Dr. Schmidt is a national certified counselor and a licensed professional counselor in North Carolina.

John M. Novak, EdD, is professor and former chair of Graduate Studies in Education at Brock University, Canada. An invited keynote speaker on six continents, Dr. Novak is the author of numerous articles, book chapters, and 10 books and monographs. He is the past president of the Society of Professors of Education.

CHAPTER ONE

Conflict and the Six-C Process

It is the start of a new workday. You are in your classroom, office, clinic, or other setting wondering what the day will be like. In particular, you are thinking about a specific student, colleague, client, parent, or other person who has become difficult for you to work with. As you think about it, you start to dread the appearance of this person. Today, you will be interacting with this person. You reflect on the conflict at hand and search within yourself for the best way to handle the situation.

Does this scenario have a familiar ring for you? To handle difficult situations such as this, many people depend on what has worked for them in the past. Others rely on luck, habit, or the ability to muddle through. This opening chapter provides a theory of practice for a specific approach to handling conflict that we call the Six-C Process. Without this theoretical foundation, the "how to" value of the Six-C Process would be misunderstood and severely limited.

INTRODUCTION

Disagreements are like fast cars. They can go from 0 to 100 mph in seconds. The same is true of human encounters. A minor difference can explode into a major conflict. These explosive encounters take place among families, communities, and nations. The purpose of this book is to offer a straightforward, ethical, measured, and effective way to understand and defuse difficult situations before explosions occur. And if they do occur, this book describes how to repair the damage and heal the wounds.

The Six-C Process focuses on six distinct and progressively more assertive levels for handling challenging situations. The Six Cs of the process represent six levels of functioning:

Concern (identifying latent and actionable concerns)

Confer (using nonthreatening signal systems to express a concern)

Consult (reviewing the situation collaboratively)

Confront (considering and giving clear warning of sanctions)

Combat (taking sustained action with logical consequences)

Conciliation (mending the wounds of combat)

Each of the Six C concepts has its own body of research and literature. The contribution of this book is that it combines and extends these concepts into a unique structure for handling challenging situations.

Your strategy in using the Six-C Process is to conserve your energy and time at the lowest level of action—*concern.* If that level fails to address the initial issue, you move upward through the higher levels (subsequent Cs) only as necessary until you reach the fifth C, *combat.* After you have concluded with combat, the final C, conciliate, is a highly valued level, one that is also valuable at the five previous levels.

As you move from simple processes to complex ones in seeking solutions, you do not abandon the less complex ones. Just because you have an algebra problem, you do not abandon basic arithmetic. All mathematical systems maintain their value and usefulness. In using the Six Cs, as you ratchet up from concern to confer, to consult, to confront, to combat, you continue to use all related processes as you become ever more direct and assertive in addressing your concern.

The Six-C Process offers a way to navigate through difficult situations in a democratic and respectful manner while conserving time and energy. By applying the philosophy and strategies of the Six-C Process, you will be in better position to act caringly and effectively in handling conflicts within your family, friendships, work, and the larger community.

While every concern has its own unique quality and flavor, the Six-C Process aims to find a desirable end for every potential conflict one might imagine, large and small, personal and professional. This includes potentially dangerous situations, which we will address in Chapters 5 and 6. Of course, many concerns and difficult situations cannot be defused, altered, solved, or molded into a satisfactory conclusion. This book is limited to troublesome human concerns where it is possible that you can obtain a desirable outcome.

RESEARCH AND ANECDOTAL SUPPORT

The Six-C Process is a relatively new model for handling conflict. Several disciplines have published research that underpins this model. For example, support comes from studies regarding the effectiveness of helping and communication skills (Egan, 2002), appropriate confrontation (Burgess & Burgess, 1996, 1997), educational leadership (Fisher, Ury, & Patton, 1991; Fisher, 2005; Ury, 2008), and difficult school environments (Purkey & Powell, 2005).

In addition, there is a growing body of anecdotal support for its usefulness, including responding to school violence (Ratledge, 2008), school discipline (Tom Carr, personal communication, July 8, 2009), and community reconciliation in Northern Ireland (William Tate, personal communication, July 20, 2009). Carr's study is instructive. His application of the Six-C Process involved teaching all students in grades three through five in an elementary school how to use the approach. The teaching included giving each child a quality plastic card listing and describing the six levels of functioning. Teachers, principal, and students reported a significant positive improvement in school relationships. Significantly, fewer students visited the counseling office with peer problems.

Other authorities have endorsed approaches that encourage systematic and measured responses to conflict situations. For example, Gladwell (2008) provided a graphic example of the importance of graduated levels of action in addressing troublesome situations. He pointed out the advantages and disadvantages of mitigated speech, which is downplaying or sugarcoating the meaning of what you are trying to communicate. You mitigate when you are overly mindful of feelings. In many situations, mitigation is entirely appropriate. In others, it can be deadly.

According to Gladwell, every airline throughout the world has a special program to teach junior crewmembers how to communicate clearly and assertively. For example, a copilot might begin with an expressed concern. "Captain, I'm concerned about . . ." If nothing happens, the copilot might move up a level and state, "Captain, I'm uncomfortable with . . ." If the captain still does not respond, the copilot confronts the pilot with, "Captain, I believe this situation is unsafe." If the confrontation does not work, the copilot is required to take command of the aircraft. As Gladwell emphasized, being deferential and polite are appropriate in most situations, but mitigation has no place in a cockpit on a stormy night, in a classroom when a disruptive student is endangering self or others, or in a mental-health clinic where a client is threatening harm.

WHAT IS UNIQUE ABOUT THIS BOOK?

Our approach differs significantly from others described in books on conflict management and conflict resolution in four significant ways.

1. The approach is anchored in democratic values.

2. It follows the perceptual tradition of understanding behavior from another individual's point of view.

3. It provides a straightforward, easy-to-follow formula for handling challenges, large and small, personal and professional.

4. It goes beyond managing or resolving conflicts by introducing the vital quality of conciliation.

Simply managing or resolving conflicts is insufficient. Moving to restore and enrich relationships is a significant action to take after a conflict has been resolved.

At the beginning, we want to emphasize that no method, skills, or process can guarantee a desirable outcome. Conflicts come in myriad forms, large and small, personal and professional. Many may be nearly impossible to ameliorate. Nevertheless, if you have a plan of action you have a decided advantage over the one who does not. Even if the ultimate result is unsuccessful, at least you know what went wrong. Without a plan, such as the Six-C Process, you are left with the guesswork of trial and error.

THE SIX-C PROCESS

The Six-C Process offers both a principled philosophy and a practical strategy for addressing challenging situations in all areas and all levels of human behavior. It offers both an overarching strategy and specific tactics for addressing challenging situations in myriad areas of human endeavor. We base this process on proper concern and respect for the dignity and worth of everyone involved.

THE CONCILIATION CAPSTONE

Conciliation is a condition infused in each of the preceding levels of the approach. As such, conciliation is a necessary ingredient at each level of the process. Diagram 1.1 illustrates the Six-C Process.

Diagram 1.1   Six-C Process

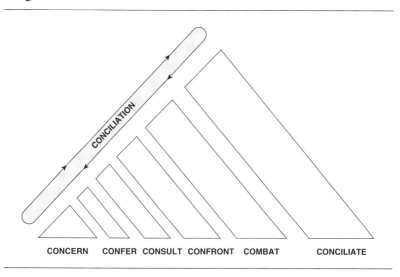

CONCERN   CONFER   CONSULT   CONFRONT   COMBAT   CONCILIATE

Key Point 1.1

Simply managing or resolving conflicts is insufficient. The Six-C Process is a way of relating to oneself, others, and the world in trusting and caring ways.

As you can see in Diagram 1.1, conciliation is the capstone of the Six-C Process. It is the sixth and essential level of the process because simply resolving a conflict is unlikely to be sufficient or satisfactory. The process assumes that it is vital to bring opposing ideas and antagonistic forces together. By working through *conciliation*, therefore, you seek to restore relationships possibly damaged by earlier efforts to resolve a concern. If not properly addressed using conciliatory processes, particular situations can extend far beyond their original conflicts. It is common to hear of unending family arguments, regional and national antagonisms, and deadly feuds, where hostilities continue long after people forget the original source of the conflict. Through conciliatory action, you rely on good will to minimize the risk of forgetfulness and reduce the residue of hatred and anger. An illustration of how hatred and anger can fester after a situation is resolved is provided by the actions of one factory owner.

> The owner was involved in an ongoing conflict with his 300 employees. It finally reached the point where the employees took the owner to court. The legal system ruled against the owner and closed the case. However, before the company mailed the December salary checks to its 300 employees, the owner took a pen and angrily scratched out the message, "Happy Holidays & Best Wishes," embossed on each of the checks.

The Six-C Process may appear too simple when compared with the myriad complexities of human conflict. However, simplicity involves cutting through complexities to uncover fundamental dynamics. The Six-C Process provides a valuable mnemonic device for understanding and addressing very complex circumstances. You can mentally process each of the Six Cs when handling specific conflicts. By doing so, you evaluate and reflect on each level to determine its effectiveness in reaching a solution. Your goal is to capture the simplicity of the process, which often exists on the other side of complexity.

SAVING TIME AND ENERGY

In moving from concern through conciliation, you want to be as *economical* as possible. In other words, avoid multiplying a potential problem unnecessarily. This does not mean that a simple explanation is always the best. It means the simplest course of action is often the most useful in addressing given circumstances and moving toward conciliation. For example, if your television set is not working, check to see if you have plugged it in before hauling it to a technician for repairs. Applying this maxim to conflict means, everything else being equal, you choose the level in working through conflict that carries the least baggage and seeks to move on amicably. In other words, don't try to kill a fly with a sledgehammer.

In any situation of possible concern, major or minor, personal or professional, where there is the possibility of conflict, the first thing to ask yourself is, "How can I successfully address this situation at the lowest possible level using the least amount of time and energy?" Take for example, the following exchange.

> *Science teacher says to the chemistry class, "Some students are not cleaning up their lab stations."*
>
> *Student replies, "Why don't you tell those students who are messy instead of blaming all of us?"*

If you were the teacher in this instance, how would you perceive the challenge from the student? What would be your response to handle the situation at the lowest possible level with the least amount of energy? Consider these two responses.

> *Science teacher says, "Thank you, (student's name). You make a good point, and I will take the action you suggest. At the same time, it may be useful for all students to hear my concern about keeping the lab clean."*
>
> *Or, the science teacher says, "Listen, I said 'some students.' Just make sure you clean up after yourself."*

Anyone can escalate a minor concern into a major conflict. A prime example of how easy it is to go from concern to combat is provided in the following scenario.

> *A spouse of one of the authors had a concern about a new rug she purchased because it had a toxic odor after the installation. She asked the company representative to visit her home and see what could be done about the smell. The spouse's daughter was visiting when the company representative arrived. He sniffed the rug and said that the odor was normal and nothing could be done. The daughter declared, "Well, we will stop payment on the carpet!" To which the representative responded, "In that case, we'll see you in court!" In a heartbeat, the rug situation had escalated from concern to combat.*

It takes special effort and desire to navigate a potential conflict effectively, efficiently, and democratically.

CONFLICT IS INEVITABLE

Conflict is inevitable because people have different wants, strategies, interests, styles, and viewpoints. It is difficult to imagine that any type of social or behavioral change could occur without some degree of conflict. According to Fullan (2001), the absence of conflict can be a sign of death. He maintains that an appreciation of the values of resistance is a remarkable discovery in a culture of constant change. Accepting this notion—that conflict is bound to happen—you will be better able to stay ahead of the conflicts in your personal life and at work.

Conflict can be beneficial. It often serves as an opportunity to enhance relationships, learn useful information, alter perceptions, and create new personal and professional directions. Handled within a particular framework, conflict can provide relatively limitless opportunities for growth. According to Forni (2008), this is particularly true if you measure success in terms of how you want things to be rather than the degree to which you defeat other people and their ideas.

Teachers, administrators, counselors, and allied professionals face the need to resolve vexing conflicts, handle difficult situations, and maintain order the same as anyone else in society, particularly in light of the tumultuous and complex nature of today's schools. We also find similar complexity and challenges in other social agencies—medical facilities, mental health clinics, and social welfare services, to name a few.

In your role as an educator or helping professional, there is no way to avoid taxing, frustrating, and even dangerous situations. You can expect to encounter stubborn students, angry parents, reluctant clients, difficult colleagues, and indifferent strangers. Regardless of the challenges, society and your profession hold you to a high standard and expect you to be a beneficial presence in the lives of students, clients, and others.

Education, if it lives up to its name, is about appreciating, understanding, and improving the human condition. Educators, if they live up to their name, model an educative approach to life. Therefore, educational modeling is especially important in situations in which perceived conflict is often difficult, disruptive, and dreaded. Such modeling applies to all of the helping professions.

Key Point 1.2

Conflict often serves as an opportunity to enhance relationships, learn useful information, alter perceptions, and create new personal and professional directions. Handled within a particular framework, conflict can provide relatively limitless opportunities for conciliation.

THE USE AND MISUSE OF POWER

Power is usually defined as the possession of control, authority, or influence over others. We use the term to suggest the ability to significantly change a situation. Power comes in myriad forms. A teacher has the power to pass or fail a student. A school superintendent has the power to hire and fire teachers. A staff member has the power to file a grievance. A parent has the power to discipline a child. A school board has the power to appoint a new principal. The public has the power to vote school board members in or out of office. A student has the power to report a teacher's misbehavior. The list is endless. However, the use of power is a double-edged sword, meaning that its use can have both favorable and unfavorable consequences.

Sometimes, you might be tempted to resolve a concern by using some form of power (physical, economic, position, dependence, withholding information and knowledge, etc.), but the use of indiscriminant power is seldom as effective or efficient as you would think. The energy you expend to exert power often does not equal the results you hope to achieve. When applying the Six-C Process, consider and recognize the types of power you have in your personal and professional life as they relate to expressing and handling your concerns.

No one is without power. Some people, such as students, may not have as much power as you, but it is dangerous to assume that they are powerless. Often, they can exert a great counterpower. Even the most timid and insecure person has power, which he or she can often use in subtly belligerent ways to impede or diminish the power you attempt to exercise. For example, silence from an insolent student can be frustrating to a teacher who is demanding a response. Some dictatorial and aggressive teachers have gotten into serious trouble when they forgot that students have infinite ways of making their lives miserable. Some of these ways are described in the book, *Teaching Class Clowns (and What They Can Teach Us)* (Purkey, 2006).

An illustration of how the use of power can backfire is the story of a school principal who wanted to dismiss the school custodian.

The principal knew that without proper cause and due process, he could not fire the custodian. One morning, the principal looked out his office window and spotted the custodian, sound asleep on a bench. The principal quickly filed the necessary charges to fire the apparently lazy custodian. When the school board reviewed the charge of sleeping on the job, it discovered that the custodian was sleeping because he had volunteered to work the night before to clean up after a broken water pipe had flooded the basement of a neighboring school. Although the school board did not condone the custodian's behavior of sleeping on the job, it understood the situation and did not fire him. In fact, they commended the custodian's willingness to go beyond the call of duty in helping a neighboring school. The Board also expressed displeasure with the principal's hasty action in trying to fire the custodian without an investigation of the entire situation.

If you only use power when addressing conflicts, you can never be certain how much to assert in a given situation. More importantly, using sheer force is contrary to the democratic ideals and strategies that guide the Six-C Process. These ideals and strategies follow a conviction that all people are valuable, able, and responsible, and they should be active participants regarding issues that affect their lives (Novak, 2002; Purkey & Novak, 1996). The use of indiscriminant power increases the risk of damaging any relationship. It also has the sinister quality of not knowing where the use of force might lead, particularly when dealing with strangers.

Bowen (in press), Bowen and Mohr (2009), and others investigated the use of coercion in psychiatric settings. They concluded that coercion is an unacceptable part of the health care milieu insofar as it diminishes the dignity of the person being coerced, elicits retaliation, and when initially effective in gaining expected power, results in further coercion on the part of the caregiver. With the above caveat, we now present two theoretical foundations of the Six-C Process—the democratic ideal and the perceptual tradition.

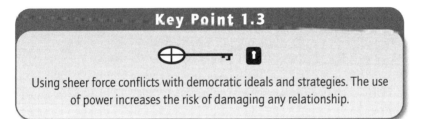

Key Point 1.3

Using sheer force conflicts with democratic ideals and strategies. The use of power increases the risk of damaging any relationship.

THE DEMOCRATIC IDEAL

As with any behavioral strategy, some people might use the Six-C Process to manipulate situations solely for their own benefit. Of course, that is not the intention. The Six-C Process works best when applied within a democratic system that respects and values all people involved in the relationship.

In moving from conflict through conciliation, the Six-C Process adheres to a democratic ideal. An ideal represents something of value that is worthy of pursuit. As active forces, democratic ideals encourage you to move along an ethical path from *what is* to *what might be* to *what should be* to *what will be* (see Diagram 1.2). There is a built-in advantage in pursuing a principled and democratic concern rather than an undemocratic and unprincipled one. Without democratic ideals, people merely maintain the status quo, pushed by external stimuli and pulled by inner impulses, wondering at times, "Is this all that there is?"

Diagram 1.2

What is
↓
What might be
↓
What should be
↓
What will be

Acting without democratic ideals and instead favoring auto-cratic tactics, people may attempt to resolve conflicts without regard for the dignity of the people involved and the fairness of the situation. Democratic ideals serve as personal and professional guides that give a sense of beneficial purpose and respectful direc-tion to day-to-day living. They also exclaim that everyone in the process has worth—everyone matters.

Key Point 1.4

As active forces, democratic ideals encourage you to move along an ethical path from *what is* to *what might be* to *what should be* to *what will be.*

WHY EVERYONE MATTERS

A democratic philosophy includes an ethical commitment to the proposition that all people matter and can participate meaning-fully in the rules and institutions that direct their lives. In schools, for example, this means that students, teachers, and others have a significant voice in determining the policies that govern their behavior. Sometimes, teachers and principals give lectures to students on "our" rules when students have not had any input on the formation of these policies. We might say the same about teachers who have had little or no say in developing their school's faculty manual.

To say that everyone matters is to include those who society traditionally ignores—the poor, the powerless, the unsuccessful, and those different from the majority. This means that students, clients, adult caregivers, and others who dress differently, speak differently, and act differently all matter.

Acting consistently with the democratic ideal in mind is eas-ier said than done. Nevertheless, acting intentionally to put this ideal into practice summons others to embrace it. This ideal is particularly important in celebrating diversity. We all like to know there are patterns we can rely on, and we all may experi-ence discomfort with the unfamiliar. As a friend noted, "One sign of maturity is the ability to be comfortable with people who are different."

To the degree that you embrace and apply democratic principles, you will be consistent in how you use the Six-C Process. The democratic ideal says that the Six-C Process is more than simply a tactic, an efficacious way of responding to conflict. Rather, it is an educationally defensible way of working with a broad range of people to resolve countless issues.

Key Point 1.5

A democratic philosophy includes an ethical commitment to the proposition that all people matter and can participate meaningfully in the rules and institutions that direct their lives.

Equally important for educators and related professionals is the insight that democracy is the preferred ideal because, as John Dewey (1916) noted, it is the most *educative* form of governance. Learning how to deal with conflict through education and without violence provides opportunities for personal growth and social stability. In contrast, attempting to teach democratic values in a dictatorial and totalitarian environment is counterintuitive and counterproductive. An ironic example might be the few uninformed school systems that continue to allow corporal punishment despite volumes of educational research that declare its ineffectiveness. Such irony is illustrated by a misguided principal who paddles an erring student while proclaiming, "This will teach you not to go around hitting other people."

Accepting democracy as a guiding ideal and an educative course is essential to intentionally applying the Six-C Process and resolving conflict in respectful, trustworthy, and optimistic ways. An important step in accepting the democratic ideal is your understanding and appreciation of the significance that people's perspective and point of view bring to any given situation. How people see the same event is often quite different, and the degree to which you accept these varying viewpoints will help determine your ability to deal with conflict.

THE PERCEPTUAL TRADITION

The Six-C Process is based on the perceptual tradition. This tradition seeks to understand humans from an internal frame of reference. In other words, what do things look like from the person's point of view? The tradition was developed in the 20th century by perceptually oriented researchers such as Jourard (1964) with self-disclosure, Maslow (1968) with self-actualization, Rogers (1951, 1980) with person-centered therapy, and Combs and Snygg (1959) with a perceptual approach to understanding behavior.

Human behavior is a function of how, at a given moment, people view themselves, others, and situations—in the past, present, and future. An illustration of this phenomenon is the highly talented student artist who refuses to enter her paintings in an art competition. Her self-image of "not being talented enough" prevents her from taking the chance of losing the competition. By not entering, she cannot lose, and more important, others will not view her art as unworthy.

The Six-C Process encourages understanding of human motivation from an internal viewpoint. Put simply, behavior is a result of each person's unique perceptions. This understanding of human behavior is different from the more commonly held point of view that it is more accurate to interpret behavior from an external perspective. Examine the following exchanges and determine which seem to take an external view or internal view of behavior. See if you agree with our responses in parentheses.

Parent to parent:	"Children from homes like that don't try very hard in school." (external)
Teacher to class:	"If you get all this work done, you will get a special treat." (external)
Student to teacher:	"I would do better work if you were not so mean to me." (external)
Client to counselor:	"All my problems are rooted in my father's indifference." (external)
Teacher to counselor:	"What might she have been feeling to do something like that?" (internal)

Parent to teacher:	"Our family is faced with many difficulties, yet we can help our children do better in school." (internal)
Teacher to principal:	"What might our curriculum look like to that student?" (internal)

An internal view of human motivation says that motivation is a given. There is only one kind of motivation—an internal and continuous incentive that every person has all the time, in all places, during all activities (Combs, Avila, & Purkey, 1978). For example, students may not do what parents and teachers would like them to do, but this does not mean that students are unmotivated. They are simply doing, from their point of view at a moment of action, the best and safest thing they can do. Consider the following illustration.

> *A teacher who hides behind an air of indifference about rigorous lesson planning, even to the point of failing to prepare adequate lessons, is doing the best and safest thing to maintain self-worth from that teacher's point of view—"It is better not to prepare than it is to be prepared and still be an ineffective teacher." From an internal perspective, the teacher is behaving in ways that are the best and safest at this particular time.*

This theory of behavioral development is important when applying the Six-C Process.

When moving through the Six Cs, you want to resolve conflicts in ways that allow people to protect their self-worth. If you accept this assumption, you can shift your energy away from a "doing to" process of trying to motivate students, clients, or others toward a "doing with" process of summoning students and others to monitor and alter their internal dialogue and choose beneficial actions (Purkey, 2000; Purkey & Schmidt, 1996; Schmidt, 2002).

Explore the following exchanges and identify the "doing to" versus "doing with" relationships. See if you agree with our analyses in parentheses.

Counselor to client:	"These are the strategies I have chosen that will work best to cure your inappropriate behavior." (doing to)

Parent to child:	"I'll carry your glass to the table, because you will spill the milk." (doing to)
Teacher to student:	"If we put our heads together, we will come up with ideas to help make math less of a drag and more fun." (doing with)
Administrator to faculty:	"What we need are creative ideas to address this conflict. Let's be open to innovative suggestions—even the most unusual notions might have merit!" (doing with)

Most relationships are successful when people work to share and understand each other's perceptions. Shared perceptions alone do not necessarily lead to conciliation of a conflict. However, by sharing and understanding different perspectives, you place yourself in a stronger position to bridge differences that invariably exist. Considering the perceptual world of the other person is more than courtesy and respect, it is necessary for meaningful communication—a key component of the Six-C Process.

Key Point 1.6

From an internal perspective, you and others behave in ways that are the best and safest at the particular moment.

WHEN VIEWPOINTS COLLIDE

During a conflict, people frequently fail to understand the various viewpoints involved. Consequently, what begins as a minor disagreement escalates into something more. Emotional investment, material loss or gain, self-preservation, or other human conditions might seem to explain this lack of understanding, but at the core, it is the inability or unwillingness to accept and understand how others view the situation that prevents positive movement and growth. For example, a student wears his baseball cap in the classroom. The teacher views the cap as a sign of disrespect. The

"Emotional Intelligence"

Daniel Goleman

1.) Self Awareness - understand yourself

2.) Self Regulation - ability to control, redirect disruptive moods and impulses. openess to change

3.) Motivation - a passion to work for a cause beyond money & status

4.) Empathy - ability to understand emotional make-up of others.

5.) Social Skill - proficiency in managing relationships and building networks, finding common ground or rapport.

student sees the cap as simply a part of his clothing—it *completes* his outfit. In a rapidly changing pluralistic world, culturally responsible education is essential. Deciding how to act on such issues requires your respectful thought and action, including an understanding of the other person's perspective.

The Six-C Process proposes that to move from conflict to conciliation it is essential for you to understand the meaningfulness of various viewpoints. With such understanding, you place yourself in a stronger position to *accept* the perceptions of those you intend to teach, assist, or lead. It also helps you distinguish between acceptance and agreement.

ACCEPTANCE VERSUS AGREEMENT

Acceptance of another's perspective does not mean agreement with that point of view. It does mean, however, that you recognize and acknowledge a person's viewpoint. Maintaining your own belief system while acknowledging and accepting the existence of another point of view takes thoughtful reflection. Such reflection allows different perspectives to coexist in harmony to achieve a greater goal.

Sometimes in the heat of a battle, we interpret conflicting behaviors and perceptions of others as "illogical," "irrational," "selfish," "wrong-headed," "disrespectful," or "insulting." Such interpretations do little to demonstrate understanding of the power of human perception. Within the internal view of human motivation, illogical behavior does not exist. This is because people always behave in ways that make the most sense to them in a given situation at the moment of their acting. Their inner logic helps preserve the belief system they hold about themselves and the world around them. Therefore, an external assessment of another person's "irresponsible," "self-defeating," or "destructive" behavior during a conflict, in and of itself, is unlikely to facilitate your resolution of the situation and movement toward conciliation. Such assessments also elicit unnecessary and unproductive arguments.

Arguing is often counterproductive. "You are wrong" can be perceived as "You are wrong, you dumb jackass." As Forni (2008) pointed out, arguing is not a smart use of time and energy. Arguments tend to escalate conflicts, encourage defensiveness, reduce flexibility, and can harm relationships.

Key Point 1.7

To move from conflict to conciliation, it is essential to understand the meaningfulness of various viewpoints. With such understanding, you place yourself in a stronger position to *accept* the perceptions of those you intend to teach, assist, or lead.

In conflicts, it is especially important for you to maintain a high level of interest in and respect for each person in the process. This can be challenging, particularly in the most difficult situations. By being an active listener, you demonstrate genuine interest for the other person. Consider the following examples.

- *A colleague struggling to manage his class says, "These students are so unruly; it doesn't seem worth my energy to prepare lesson plans." You might respond, "Managing class behavior is challenging. Are you saying that the lesson plans you develop are not helping to keep your students engaged and attentive?"*
- *A client trying to overcome a particular anxiety reports to the counselor, "If I try not to think about spiders in my house as you suggested, I'll probably become anxious about something else." The counselor might reply, "Yes, there are many things in life to worry about. Together, we can address your arachnophobia, or we can focus on other worries. What do you think?"*
- *The school principal says, "The teachers most worthy of my assistance have the desire to improve. Whereas it seems like I am running up against a brick wall with teachers that don't care." A supervisor might answer, "I agree that teachers offer a range of ability and desire. That is what challenges you as their principal. What might be the outcome if you worked only with those who have the most potential for change?"*

These examples offer a brief opportunity to consider how the use of active listening might remedy conflicts. You can see that implicit in each example are perceptions that color the situation. Perhaps you can think of better responses than those in the examples. How you respond to words spoken as well as the implied perceptions behind them will determine your success in handling difficult situations.

You can see from the examples above that moving from conflict to conciliation is facilitated by some knowledge of basic helping skills. Listening and other helpful behaviors that communicate acceptance, empathy, and commitment by all involved in conflict situations are great assets to the process. Because the focus of this book prevents a detailed explanation of helping skills, we encourage you to explore books on professional counseling. Texts by Egan (2002), Gross and Capuzzi (2007), Kottler (2008), Meier and Davis (1993), Purkey and Schmidt (1996), and Schmidt (2002) are examples that provide detailed explanations of helping skills.

Before moving to the next chapters that describe each of the Six Cs, a cautionary note is appropriate. We intend the Six-C Process for people who are essentially healthy functioning individuals, free of psychopathology and other serious, incapacitating dysfunction. Therefore, the Six-C Process is an optimistic approach balanced by a realistic perspective. It does not replace appropriate psychological, medical, or other interventions designed to handle serious cases of dysfunctional human relationships.

Key Point 1.8

It is especially important to maintain a high level of interest and respect for each person in the process. This can be challenging, particularly in the most difficult situations.

SUMMARY

This opening chapter presented an introduction to the Six-C Process and its foundations, the democratic ideal, and the perceptual tradition. The democratic ideal described democracy as a function of education and collaboration. In a democracy, everyone matters.

The perceptual tradition maintains that what a person believes to be true about self and others is as important as how he or she behaves. Of particular importance is the relationship between perceptions and conflict. In applying the Six-C Process, you increase your chances of success to the extent that you understand this relationship.

Each of the following chapters addresses and explores one of the six powerful Cs in turn (concern, confer, consult, confront, combat, and conciliate). Effective actions involved with each level are presented, beginning with the first level, *concern*.

Major Themes

- Conflict is an inevitable and inescapable part of life. How you perceive the personal and professional conflicts that you encounter, and the skills with which you deal with these situations, will enhance your chances to achieve a desirable outcome.
- The Six-C Process is a practical structure for moving from concern through conciliation. A principal belief of the Six-C Process is that you will be most successful in dealing with conflict when you begin at the lowest level of intervention and move upward only as necessary.
- A disposition for genuine and effective communication that conveys interest in and respect for other people helps you deal with conflict. How you listen, empathize, and respond to others is fundamental in using the Six-C Process.

CHAPTER TWO

Concern

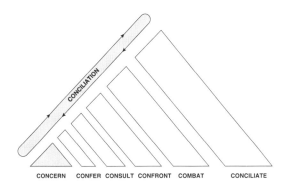

CONCERN CONFER CONSULT CONFRONT COMBAT CONCILIATE

During free periods in the teachers' workroom, a fellow teacher often uses profanity. You would prefer that he not use this sort of language in your presence. Is this a preference or a concern? Should you say anything about his language, and if so, when is the right time and where is an appropriate place to express your concern?

*C*oncern is the first level in the Six-C Process. The word, concern, has several definitions. We focus on concern as something that matters to the person experiencing it and negatively affects someone or a group of people. Concern often takes the form of an uneasy feeling of blended sadness, anger, indignation, or fear. This chapter explores the nature and sources of concern, including moral and ethical reasons why you may or may not decide to be concerned over a particular situation.

LATENT CONCERNS

Before exploring the nature and sources of concern, we distinguish between two types of concerns that indicate potential conflict. The first type is *latent concerns.* These concerns are situations that you encounter, and after brief consideration, you decide they do not require immediate attention or action. You observe the situation and store information away, planning to watch for future developments. You take no steps to intervene at this time. For example, a latent concern might be observing a colleague who predictably comes late to team meetings. You wonder if it is fair to the people who are always on time. Yet, your colleague's lack of punctuality in this matter does not interfere with the productivity of the team, so as a member of the team you ignore it for the time being.

Another example of a latent concern might be that of a fellow teacher who brings her lunch to school to eat in the teachers' lounge. The smell of the food is very strong and unpleasant to you. You might think to yourself, "If this becomes a chronic and recurring concern, I might say something. Meanwhile, I'll wait and see how her future lunches are."

Latent concerns often disappear in time. When they persist, however, or become more worrisome, you might want to move them to another category, one that requires you to do something.

ACTIONABLE CONCERNS

The second type of concern is an *actionable concern.* In these instances, your assessment helps you to conclude that you must express your concern and take other action if necessary. Your actionable concern might be noticing that a colleague spends an unusual amount of time after school with a particular student in her office with the door shut and blinds drawn. A second example of an actionable concern would be a student who often interrupts other students during class presentations and discussions. The student may not know that his behavior is annoying. Nevertheless, the rudeness calls for action. Throughout this book, you will want to think about *latent* and *actionable concerns* as you review examples and contemplate conflicts in your personal and professional life.

You might guess that a range of feelings occurs in many forms when contemplating latent and actionable concerns. Recognizing your particular emotions during these encounters can provide you with greater understanding of the concern itself. It will also help you to control your emotions, particularly when the other person does not do what you want. Considering all these feelings and related factors takes time and effort.

An essential characteristic of the Six-C Process is to use time efficiently. One way to use time efficiently is to avoid making snap decisions and moving too fast to a higher-level C. Take time to reflect on a concern before you decide to move to a more assertive C level. Moving too quickly through the Six-C Process, like drinking wine before it has properly aged, can be counterproductive and self-defeating (or distasteful). Should you have the luxury of time, take it.

WHAT IS A CONCERN?

When considering whether a situation is a concern, it is helpful to ask yourself some questions. By asking yourself specific questions about the concern, you can better determine whether a situation is truly a matter of concern, and if so, to what degree. Here are ten questions to ask yourself when evaluating a potential concern:

1. Is the concern about safety and welfare?

2. Is the situation truly a concern?

3. If a concern does exist, will it resolve itself?

4. Can you overlook the concern?

5. Can you do anything about the concern?

6. Can you reconceptualize the concern?

7. Is this the right time and place to be concerned?

8. Does the concern simply annoy you?

9. Is the concern due to personal prejudices or biases?

10. Does the concern involve morals and ethics?

It will be helpful to consider briefly each of these questions.

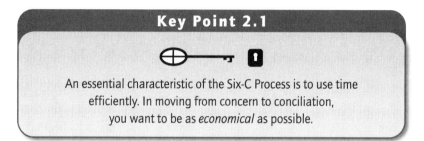

Key Point 2.1

An essential characteristic of the Six-C Process is to use time efficiently. In moving from concern to conciliation, you want to be as *economical* as possible.

Question 1: Is the concern about safety and welfare?

The safety and welfare of people are always legitimate concerns and a *top priority* to consider before moving forward with the Six-C Process. As examples, educators are morally, ethically, and legally responsible for the safety and welfare of students. Similarly, therapists adhere to ethical principles with their clients, as do medical personnel with their patients.

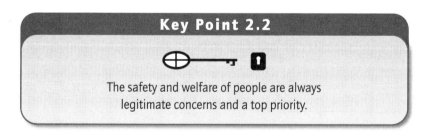

Key Point 2.2

The safety and welfare of people are always legitimate concerns and a top priority.

In schools and other locations, dismantling a smoke detector, covering glass windows in classroom doors, blocking a fire door, or removing warning signs are clearly matters of concern. Likewise, a counselor who places clients at undue risk when suggesting new behaviors without providing the necessary precautions raises ethical and legal concerns.

Question 2: Is the situation truly a concern?

Once you have addressed the question of safety, the next thought that should come to mind when using the Six-C Process is to ask yourself, "Is this really a matter of concern?" There are some smaller questions embedded in this larger one. For example, what do things look like from the other person's point of view? Could it be that your viewpoint is distorted or in error? What is really going on here? How far am I willing to go with this concern? Is "winning" an argument more important to you than resolving the concern in a mutually desirable manner? As an illustration, you might prefer that students dress better when they come to school, but it may not be a concern. Having the desire for something to happen or a situation to be different is not necessarily a concern.

Individuals form their opinions based on present circumstances and predicted future possibilities as influenced by their experiences. Often, what at first blush appears to be a concern is simply a preference. To illustrate, one of the authors of this book prefers to be called "William" rather than "Bill," but it is not a concern. He does not object to a more familiar name; he simply prefers the more-formal nomenclature. (This may have something to do with his childhood. When the postman delivered the mail, his mother would often say, "Not another bill!")

A potential concern may even dissolve into a source of classroom humor. A silly wisecrack from a class clown in response to a teacher's question might be more of an occasion for mutual laughter than a concern. One of the authors (Purkey, 2006) has written a book describing encounters, good and bad, in working with class clowns. He describes an event when a middle school principal visited a classroom to observe and evaluate the teacher's skills. The teacher, anxious to impress the principal with her knowledge of pedagogy, diagramed a sentence on the board and then asked the class if anyone knew why she had done this. The resident class clown responded, "Yeah, it's because the principal's sitting there." Keeping a good sense of humor is critical in teaching these humorous students.

Question 3: If a concern does exist, will it resolve itself?

Frequently, the passage of time will resolve a concern. (Overbearing houseguests eventually go home. Disgruntled colleagues sometimes relocate or retire.) Time has a way of putting things in perspective. Many concerns take care of themselves. For example, experienced teachers will ignore student horseplay at the beginning of class, knowing that the students will settle down when teachers begin the lessons.

Here is another experience by one of the authors illustrating how time can solve a concern.

> Recently, I visited a friend's home. I brought a lollipop (sweet on a stick) for their young, toddler-age daughter. The little girl was delighted with the gift, but when she attempted to unwrap her lollipop, she had difficulty. She tried several times without success. Many parents would have jumped in at this point and unwrapped the candy for the little girl, but not my friend. He sat quietly and watched his daughter struggle with the wrapping. I also wanted to rush in and unwrap the lollipop, but I followed my friend's lead and did nothing. Finally, the little girl got her lollipop unwrapped. She held it up for all to see, and with a radiant smile proclaimed, "I did it myself!" What this meant to me is that when chances of success are good, it may be best to encourage people to unwrap their own lollipops.

The above examples illustrate the notion that sometimes the concerns you have will dissipate without any direct action on your part. This does not mean that you are able to ignore all types of concerns, but at least ask yourself, "Does it require action on my part at this time?"

Question 4: Can you overlook the concern?

It is psychologically unhealthy to be concerned about everything all the time. It is equally true that consistently ignoring legitimate concerns will bring significant stress. Your goal is to find a happy balance among competing perceptions.

Key Point 2.3

When you solve problems for people that they can solve for themselves, it might be a counterproductive strategy. It can encourage dependency when autonomy is a more appropriate goal.

One of the authors and his wife take a walk almost every day in a beautiful park. Every so often, they encounter three runners coming from the opposite direction. The path is narrow and so the author and wife must step aside for the three runners. Stepping aside is a momentary bother, but it is not a concern. In fact, it is a source of humor. They laugh it off.

Stress is a given in most lives. Making the decision about what to overlook without bringing additional stress to your life is an individual and personal choice. Learning your level of tolerance for everyday inconveniences and annoyances may be the first step to take in determining what concerns to place on hold (latent) and on which to act (actionable).

Question 5: Can you do anything about the concern?

There are some situations where all the concern in the world will not change things. For example, suppose a child is born with a shriveled arm. It is highly unlikely that anything could be done about the arm itself. Rather than focusing on the child's unique arm and the challenges it presents, it may be more productive and powerful to attend to concerns that are manageable for the welfare of the child and the adult caregivers.

Key Point 2.4

It is psychologically unhealthy to be concerned about everything all the time. It is equally true that consistently ignoring legitimate concerns will bring significant stress.

Another aspect of the question whether you can do anything about a concern is to examine what you are willing to do to alter the situation *versus* what changes you expect the other person to make. Sometimes, you might wonder why certain people cannot or will not change their views or behaviors. You think, "If only this person would act differently, I would not be so concerned." Adlerian theorists suggest that one way to bring about change in a relationship is for you to make changes in yourself (Sweeney, 1998). For example, a teacher concerned about a student's misbehavior in class, might see if any change in his or her behavior toward this student might help bring about desired outcomes. You can take control of your own behavior more easily and efficiently than you could ever control the behavior of others. Determining what is or is not a concern ultimately establishes your success or failure in handling challenging situations.

Question 6: Can you reconceptualize the concern?

As noted above, what people say internally has a powerful impact on how they approach situations. For example, rather than say, "I've lost my car keys," you might reconceptualize this situation to say, "I have misplaced my car keys." Cognitive theorists call this "reframing." It is a process of rethinking and restating problematic situations (George & Cristiani, 1995).

Key Point 2.5

Determining what is or is not a concern becomes part of your internal dialogue and ultimately establishes your success or failure in handling challenging situations. Changing your internal dialogue often changes your perceptions.

In reframing, it is helpful to assume that others are well meaning and have reasons for their actions. For instance, imagine that you are bothered about a new neighbor parking her car on the sidewalk rather than on her sloping driveway. You think it is inconsiderate for someone to block the sidewalk so others cannot use it. When you express your dismay to another neighbor, you learn that the new neighbor is a war veteran and double amputee who walks only with prosthetics. It is much easier for her to get in and out of her specially equipped car when it is parked on a flat surface, such as the sidewalk. You instantly reframe your concern from consternation to compassion.

Veteran teachers know how to use student energy and talent in productive ways. It is not coincidental that teachers often select some of the more troublesome students as hall monitors, ground's keepers, computer technicians, safety patrol officers, and other responsible roles. These positions give a broad range of students some responsibilities that they might otherwise not experience. To the point made here, creation of these roles for students was possible because someone, perhaps a teacher, reconceptualized how to help students take responsibility.

Question 7: Is this the right time and place to be concerned?

The advice, "Praise in public, criticize in private," makes good sense and is applicable when expressing a concern. It is also wise to wait until tempers have cooled before expressing a concern. Most people would be embarrassed to have their manners corrected in public. A case in point was provided by a high school football coach.

The coach said that several of his players fumbled the ball during a game. These fumbles probably cost the team a victory. The team was disappointed and demoralized by the defeat. Rather than "chew out" his players, the coach praised the team for the valiant effort and unwavering commitment. He knew the team felt bad enough without his critical comments. He would wait until the next practice to tell his players, "Remember the basics—Hang on to the darn ball!"

A companion factor in considering time and place is to consider the consequences of expressing concern to another person. Sharing a concern, if you need to share it, should take into consideration the effects on the person at that moment. Just because something is on your mind does not mean it has to come out of your mouth.

Agesilaus II, ancient King of Sparta, said, "It is circumstances and proper timing that give an action its character and make it either good or bad" (quoted in *Plutarch's Lives*, Dryden & Clough, 1977). Similarly, great comedians commonly believe that good timing is the difference between having a joke fall flat or making the audience roll with laughter. Part of reconceptualizing your concern may be to consider the time and place in which to express it.

Question 8: Does the concern simply annoy you?

In a democratic society, you have the right not to be bugged. The expectation is that all people are treated with respect. Far more than a privilege, it is a basic right that everyone be treated with dignity. A democratic culture demonstrates clear concern when people are teased, bullied, ridiculed, insulted, or otherwise mistreated. What is important to know when considering personal stress is that a concern may be raised when anyone is at risk or is experiencing stress.

Here is an incident of mild stress recalled by one of the authors. One of the departmental secretaries began to call him, "Dr. Turkey." At first, it seemed to be harmless fun, but the frequent repetition of this greeting soon became bothersome to the point where the professor respectfully, efficiently, and successfully addressed the concern using the Six-C Process, which we will explain in Chapter 3. Everyone has the right not to be bothered by thoughtless, insensitive, and annoying remarks.

Question 9: Is the concern due to personal prejudices or biases?

Hatred, ignorance, frustration, and other factors sometimes contribute to people's concerns. Personal prejudices and biases frequently propel people to express concern about issues inherently harmless. By doing so, such people demonstrate their own hang-ups and personal flaws.

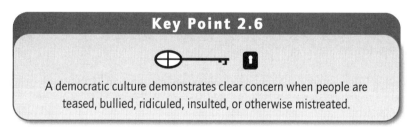

Key Point 2.6

A democratic culture demonstrates clear concern when people are teased, bullied, ridiculed, insulted, or otherwise mistreated.

To illustrate, a racist administrator may show concern about hairstyles of some students through ridicule, biased rules, inappropriate humor, or gossip. During the early days of school desegregation in the United States, a few educators complained bitterly over the "Afro" hairstyles of some African American students. Some students were even expelled from school and denied an education because of their hair. At the same time, students of the dominant race wore fluffy bouffant hairstyles without complaint from teachers or repercussion from administrators. A friend of the authors summarized it bluntly, "Make sure that you are not mixing your own racist, sexist, homophobic garbage with your concern."

Question 10: Does the concern involve morals and ethics?

This question is so critical it will receive detailed attention in the next section. In democratic relationships, moral and ethical principles govern all behavior.

WHAT ARE MORAL AND ETHICAL CONCERNS?

There are inevitable tensions and opportunities that occur in a democratic society. Schools offer countless examples of this. People do many things that others like or dislike. They smile or frown, dress well or poorly, root for a particular team or cheer for its opponent. Only some of the time do these behaviors become issues of moral concern.

Moral and ethical concerns deal with questions of perceived right or wrong. They originate and perpetuate according to the customs of a person's country and judgments of the community and larger society. Sometimes, morals take an unusual turn. Cannibalism is considered a moral imperative in a cannibalistic world. Similarly, racial segregation is a moral right in a racist society. Before the Civil War in the United States, some religious leaders advocated slavery as "God's will." None of these examples fits the moral standard of a democratic relationship, which values all human life and freedom.

In a democratic society, it is likely you will experience moral concern when you observe a violation of a basic principle. For example, your moral warning light turns on when

- A basic principle is violated (i.e., observing a person steal, lie, cheat, or hurt oneself or others);
- Negative consequences are likely to occur (i.e., spending excessive money on school athletics takes away money from academics); or
- A responsibility to care is neglected (i.e., ignoring the needs of students with learning difficulties).

In sum, a moral concern involves instances when a person's behavior is intentionally or unintentionally antisocial and destructive. Such disinviting actions communicate messages that other people are unable, incapable, and worthless. They become obstacles to human fulfillment.

It is the responsibility of concerned and caring educators and helping professionals to speak out and take action when a disturbing situation presents itself. In schools, this means people, places, policies, and programs that intentionally or unintentionally humiliate, hurt, or deny the rights of others are wrong despite evidence that these undemocratic forces might promote desired outcomes. Our position is that the ends do not justify the means. As Kidder (2005) pointed out, acting on this position often takes moral courage. We believe you can develop this courage through conscientious reflection and practice.

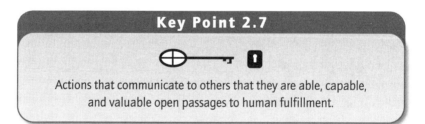

Key Point 2.7

Actions that communicate to others that they are able, capable, and valuable open passages to human fulfillment.

Reflection on moral intuition is necessary because at times a person's "moral lights" can be hair triggered or dysfunctional. Hair-triggered moral warning lights see moral violations everywhere and consequently turn on too often. Dysfunctional warning lights are often dim or too difficult to turn on in the first place. By thinking seriously and acting compassionately on complex concerns, you adhere to an important part of the journey from conflict to conciliation.

In addition to situations involving right versus wrong, other types of concern involve tensions between *right versus right.* These ethical dilemmas focus on patterns of contested rights. To illustrate, a right versus right conflict may involve the following school examples:

- *Truth Versus Loyalty.* Speaking in a straightforward manner about school difficulties versus promoting a school's reputation.
- *Individual Versus Community.* Placing a behaviorally challenged student in a regular classroom versus not disrupting the teaching and learning process for others.
- *Short Term Versus Long Term.* Teaching to the test versus building on students' interests and questions.
- *Justice Versus Mercy.* Automatically applying a zero-tolerance policy versus examining the uniqueness of a situation in which an improving student has inadvertently violated a rule.
- *Privacy Versus Security.* Respecting the right to be left alone versus searching people indiscriminately.
- *Personal Versus Professional.* Being religiously opposed to teaching sex education versus following mandated school-board policy.

Each of the above illustrations involves a challenge between ethical opinions. Being able to handle this stress requires the ability and willingness to develop what Kidder (1996) calls ethical fitness. Similar to physical fitness, which enhances your strength, flexibility, and endurance, ethical fitness is a strengthening of key components of ones' sensitivity, reasoning, and imagination.

WHAT ARE YOUR CONCERNS?

As noted in this chapter, you can put off some concerns (latent) until later, while others require your immediate attention (actionable). Fortunately, the great majority of concerns are simply a mundane part of everyday living. However, allowing some of these small concerns to simmer without resolution can result in major problems later.

Now that *concern* has been explained as the first level of intervention in the Six-C Process, and you have considered latent and actionable concerns, it is time to try an exercise to see how you identify various concerns. Perceived concerns vary greatly among individuals. Given the same situation, one individual might have no concern, another might view it as a latent concern, and a third person might take immediate action.

Reflect on the following lists of potential concerns encountered at school, home, and the larger community. What would be your level of concern about each, and how would your perceptions compare with those of colleagues, family members, and others? As you read each of the events, check them either as not a concern, a latent concern, or an actionable concern. As you do this exercise, you may realize that various concerns have temporal and situational elements that could alter how you perceive them. Timing and other factors might cause you to check a particular concern as latent one time but check the same concern as actionable at another time.

When considering the following concerns, it may be interesting to ask a colleague, friend, or relative to independently complete the survey. A comparison of viewpoints may generate valuable insights and discussion.

Potential Concerns at School

	Not a Concern	Latent Concern	Actionable Concern
• Seeing students with unusual hairstyles			
• Finding that a colleague left the copy machine empty of paper			
• Noticing that someone took two parking spaces in the faculty parking lot			
• Finding that a student has cheated on a test			

- Seeing two students of the same sex holding hands

- Seeing two students of the opposite sex holding hands

- Hearing a student make a joke at a teacher's expense

- Hearing a colleague or student use a racial slur

- Colleagues placing unwashed dishes in the faculty room sink

- Noticing a student sleeping in class

- Watching colleagues ignore a speaker at a faculty meeting

- Observing a school secretary being rude to a visitor

- Having a colleague who is overly friendly

- Noticing that furniture is blocking a fire door

- Observing a student running in the hallway

- Noticing that a colleague covers the window of a classroom or office door

- Colleagues using cell phones or text messaging during a committee meeting

Reflect on your perceptions of these potential school concerns. As you review them, consider how time, place, or other factors might influence your decisions about each. Now consider the next two lists at home and in the community.

Potential Concerns at Home

	Not a Concern	Latent Concern	Actionable Concern
Kids leaving their bicycles in the driveway			
Hearing a relative make a sexist comment			
Children encouraging the family dog to bark			
Siblings borrowing clothing without asking			
Using bad manners at the dinner table			
Flushing a toilet when someone is taking a shower			
Borrowing the car and leaving the gas tank near empty			
Chewing gum loudly			
Overloading electrical outlets			
Flipping television channels constantly when others are also watching			
Hearing a houseguest tell obscene jokes			
Seeing a relative spank a child			
Receiving a sales call during dinner			

- Being corrected in front of guests

- Seeing a guest light up a cigar

Potential Concerns in the Community

	Not a Concern	Latent Concern	Actionable Concern
Talking loudly on a cell phone			
Driving slowly in the passing lane			
Listening to a neighbor's constantly barking dog			
Finding luggage on an empty chair in a crowded airport			
Neglecting to use turn signals			
Not wearing a seat belt in a car			
Presenting 15 items at a 10-item checkout counter			
Talking in a theater during a movie			
Letting a door close on someone directly behind you			
Allowing children to ride in cars without wearing seat belts			

- Writing a check in a cash-only line

- Experiencing road rage from another driver

- Littering, including trash and personal waste

- Having a child kick the back of your seat on an airplane

- Breaking the line at a theatre

- Collecting money or soliciting at traffic intersections

Key Point 2.8

Some concerns require tough choices, while with others it is an easy call. You can put off some concerns until later, while others require your immediate attention.

The above lists of circumstances are samples of the many potential concerns, significant and insignificant, that we encounter every day, at school, at home, and in the larger community. By exploring these three checklists of possible concerns, you determine how you might react in similar situations. Is it a concern or not? Each of the above situations involves a choice. Even when you decide a situation is *not* a concern, that decision is still a choice.

SUMMARY

In this chapter, we defined *concern* and explained its role in the Six-C Process to move successfully from conflict through conciliation.

We presented two central ideas. The first emphasized economy of time and effort in handling difficult situations. The second suggested ways to determine whether a situation is truly a concern. The chapter concluded with a sample list of potential concerns, large and small. Chapter 3 will explain the second vital C in the Six-C Process. Once you make a decision that a situation is a concern and that further action is definitely required, the second C of the Six-C Process is justified. This C is *confer.*

Major Themes

- Recognizing that you have a concern is the first and lowest level of dealing with conflict. It allows you to examine and evaluate your concern, determining whether any action is necessary at the time.
- Knowing and understanding your concern is the initial step in determining whether or not to express it openly. Answering questions for yourself about the nature of the concern and whether it is important enough to take action helps you keep things in perspective.
- In democratic relationships, moral and ethical concerns have particular significance. By becoming aware of your personal and professional ethics, you place yourself in a better position to take dependable stances on important issues and maintain a democratic posture in all your relationships.

Confer

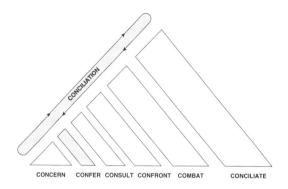

CONCERN   CONFER CONSULT CONFRONT COMBAT   CONCILIATE

Imagine that you are an elementary school principal taking a stroll around the campus. During your walk, you happen to spot the school custodian behind the trash compacter on the edge of campus taking a smoking break. Smoking on school grounds is a violation of the school district's personnel policy. What would you do?

The second level of the Six-C Process, conferring, begins with your decision that a legitimate concern exists and it is time for you to take action. The task now is to seek voluntary and mutual agreement in reaching a desired outcome.

The history of the word *confer* is interesting. It originates with the Latin, *conferre*, which means to bring together to compare views and take council. The goal of conferring is to seek an agreement in resolving a situation to the mutual satisfaction of all parties. As a proverb reminds us, "Why cut a rope that can easily be untied?" Getting results through cooperation and mutual respect is a reoccurring theme of this book.

An example of defusing conflict through conferring is provided by an episode in the classic television series Happy Days. The series featured two teenage characters Richie and Fonzie. In one of the episodes, Richie's father told him to bring Fonzie to their home for Thanksgiving dinner. (Fonzie lived alone in a tiny one-room apartment.) When Fonzie declined the offer, Richie's dad tried ordering Fonzie to accept the offer for dinner. If you remember the show Happy Days, you will recall that no one ordered "The Fonz" to do anything. When Richie's dad persisted, Fonzie began to bristle. A conflict was rapidly approaching. At that moment, Richie stepped in and defused the situation by explaining, "Fonzie, this is an invitation, Dad is inviting you to dinner" Fonzie thought for a moment, then replied, "Oh, well, if it's an invitation, I accept."

Key Point 3.1

The goal of conferring is to seek voluntary agreement in resolving a situation to the mutual satisfaction of all parties.

SETTING THE STAGE FOR CONFERRING

Before beginning the conferring process, it will be useful to review a point we made in Chapter 1. We emphasized the importance of practicing economy with concerns. Being concerned about everything all the time is a definition of mental distress. It can lead to psychological and even physical problems. When conferring, therefore, you want to use as little energy, time, and emotion as possible to reach your intended goal.

As a final checklist before conferring, it is useful to ask yourself three questions:

1. Can you express your concern clearly?

2. Can you look beyond the immediate concern?

3. Is there room for compromise or reconceptualization?

Each question helps you examine how conferring will address your concern in an efficient and expeditious manner.

Question 1: Can you express your concern clearly?

Before conferring, it is important to be aware of exactly what you want. This is particularly significant when multiple concerns are fighting for attention. Too often, people assume that their concern was expressed clearly when, in fact, it never was. This is particularly true when you signal a concern in such a subtle way that the other person overlooks or misunderstands it. You will recall that in Chapter 1 we explored the advantages and disadvantages of mitigated speech. Consider the following.

> *Some years ago, one of the authors was counseling a married couple that was having difficulties. During one session, the husband said to his wife, "I ask you to make love, but you're never interested." The wife looked puzzled and inquired, "How do you ask?" To which the husband responded, "I say, 'I'm going upstairs to take a hot bath.'" From the wife's surprised reaction, it was obvious that she was unaware of the husband's concern.*

Signaling your concern with imprecise language or ambiguous behavior places the person with whom you have the concern at a disadvantage. Saying that you are going upstairs to take a hot bath might mean simply that!

Key Point 3.2

Too often, people assume that their concern was expressed clearly when, in fact, it never was. This is particularly true when you signal a concern in such a subtle way that it is overlooked or misunderstood by the other party.

In many social circumstances, mitigated speech that avoids bluntness is entirely appropriate. At other times, straight talk is valuable. It is essential to be clear about what you are requesting. If you don't ask clearly and directly for what you want, you are not likely to get it.

A way that your communication might be ineffective is to overload the process. Too much information is as potentially damaging as too little. There are numerous examples where an excess of information masks vital messages. For example, have you ever fully read a *Truth in Lending* statement from a mortgage broker? Few of us ever do: It's too much information.

Unfortunately, for some people, miscommunication may be more deliberate than accidental. Schaub (1991) investigated the power of what he called poor communication. Withholding feelings, information, and knowledge is an effective way to deny power to perceived opponents. Some effects of poor communication include avoiding delivery of bad news (messengers often lose their heads) and avoiding confrontation (to suppress such feelings as fear, anger, or sadness) and deliberately sabotaging a situation (withholding vital information). Faced with such possibilities, you would be wise to value clear and unequivocal straight talk. Using understandable and nonaccusatory language to communicate your awareness and clarification of a perceived conflict is essential.

Key Point 3.3

It is essential to be clear about what you are requesting.

Question 2: Can you look beyond the immediate concern?

It is easy to become concerned about almost everything all the time. It is equally true that failure to address a legitimate concern can be equally damaging. For example, there are clear school rules and policies that must be followed by everyone. Failure to do so could result in expulsion of students or termination of faculty and staff. Waiting too long to express a legitimate concern can bottle up your feelings to the point where an explosion of emotion can occur. To illustrate, imagine a fellow teacher in an elementary school who leaves dirty dishes in the faculty workroom. As a colleague, you wash the dishes and say nothing. But, the latent concern simmers. Each day, you wash the dishes. Each day, your anger mounts. Finally, without warning, you blurt out to the other teacher, "You always leave dirty dishes, why are you such a pig?" Obviously, this is a poor way of working with colleagues.

Do not wait too long to confer about a legitimate concern—turn a latent concern into an actionable one. By measuring the nature of your concerns with specific criteria, such as the 10 questions presented in Chapter 2, you place yourself in a stronger position to take action regarding the concern, handling it economically and effectively.

Sometimes, concerns simply disappear or dissolve when subjected to reflection and mutual understanding of pertinent perceptions. They go away because you are able to see beyond them to what is more important in a relationship. One of the authors recounts a time when a concern of regional identity disappeared during a boyhood friendship.

He grew up on Long Island, New York, during the era when one of the fiercest rivalries in professional baseball was between the New York Yankees and the Brooklyn Dodgers. Many friendships were tested and neighborhoods divided because of loyalty to one of these teams. As a boy, he and his family vacationed in Florida, where he befriended a young native of the Sunshine State. Early in their relationship, the Floridian asked, "Are you a Yankee?" To which the New Yorker replied, "No, I'm a Dodger!" Puzzled, the southerner shook his head, while the northerner shrugged his shoulders. Unable to clarify the potential concern, the two young athletes looked beyond it and searched for other companions to play a baseball game.

Possibly, the perceived concern may be resolved by determining that it has little or no support. Ask yourself, "Am I willing to go to a higher C level if necessary?" Sometimes, it is best just to walk away and, as the comedian Jackie Gleason used to say, "Leave it to the sweepers." It is possible that your concern, upon reflection, is not worth the bother.

With some actionable concerns, time is not available for reflection. For example, if a school fire exit is locked, immediate action is required. However, with concerns of a nonemergency nature, it is helpful to consider that time is usually on your side. It is best to pace yourself whenever possible. Also, keep in mind that nonacceptance is not the same as rejection. Often, people need time to reflect before committing to an action. A personal story might explain.

A retired colleague of one of the authors provided an example of the significance of time. The retiree had lost his wife and lived alone. One day, the author invited the retired colleague to come to the author's home for dinner. When he received the invitation, the elderly gentleman "hemmed and hawed" and did not accept the cordial summons. Consequently, the author's family assumed that the retired colleague had declined their invitation. That is, until the evening of the scheduled dinner. The retired colleague knocked on the door, ready to dine. When asked about the mix-up in understanding, he stated, "Well, I didn't say I wasn't coming."

Question 3: Is there room for compromise or reconceptualization?

In preparing to address your concern, listen carefully for ways to encourage honest communication and possible compromise. For example, it may be possible to reconceptualize the entire situation. (As in a case of a colleague borrowing your stapler without asking permission. You might buy a stapler and present it as a gift to your colleague.) Remember the adage, "Flexibility is strength, rigidity is weakness." Consider a student running in the hall. He may be dashing for class because a previous class, located in another part of the school, ran late. A flexible and creative administrator might get the faculty to address this scheduling problem with innovative solutions. It would be a systematic way to encourage students to walk in the hallways.

To illustrate reconceptualization, imagine that you are a teacher and have two boys in class who insist on claiming the only window desk. It overlooks the athletic field. No compromise, such as sharing the desk at intervals, pleases them both. After reflection, you rearrange the chairs in the classroom so there are now two desks by the window. One desk for each boy. Problem solved—for the time being!

Compromises such as those suggested above are often an attractive and beneficial alternative to conflict. Reasonable compromise or reconceptualization conserves energy; unreasonable compromise brings resentment and wastes energy. By conserving energy, you are also in better position to recognize the limits of your power, which we emphasized in Chapter 1.

The Six-C Process encourages you to seek alternatives to power plays when soliciting the cooperation of others. Cooperation means a willingness to seek commitment from people whose help you want in addressing a particular concern.

THE VALUE OF SEEKING COMMITMENT

Commitment begins with recognition that a concern exists and that you appreciate the relationship you have with the person of concern. It continues with your assessment of the concern's significance and your ability to express it openly to the person or persons involved. These four conditions—recognition of a concern, desire for a respectful relationship, assessment of the concern's impact, and ability to express the concern—help you decide how to handle this actionable concern.

Optimism is a valued attribute when seeking commitment. By being optimistic about resolving the concern, you set an encouraging tone and demonstrate your commitment to seeing the process through to an acceptable conclusion. Such optimism is grounded in the reality of "what is possible," rather than an unbridled belief that "anything will work" or "anything will be acceptable" to all involved. By being optimistic, rather than cynical, you begin conferring by encouraging the commitment of everyone to the process. An illustration of the value of determined optimism was provided by a teacher.

The teacher said the radiators in her classroom were not putting out enough heat. She went to her principal and requested that the radiators be repaired. The principal replied that all maintenance work was done during the summer months when school was not in session. The teacher left the office unsatisfied with the principal's response. One week later, she returned to the principal's office and made the same request. The principals said, "Didn't I tell you that repairs were made during the summer?" The teacher replied, "Yes, but that was last week. I thought by now you would have figured out a way to have the radiators repaired." The principal relented and the radiators were promptly repaired. It often pays to be optimistically persistent about getting things done.

Another behavior that demonstrates your commitment in resolving conflicts includes *sharing responsibility.* By sharing responsibility, you help people commit to a joint effort in resolving differences so that one person is not solely responsible for the outcome. This is a major element of the Six-C Process, which views the successful resolution of a concern as a joint effort. Consequently, throughout the implementation of this second level of the Six-C Process, it is essential that you share responsibility with all involved. Although you may have expressed the original concern, reaching a suitable resolution at the conferring level requires attention and commitment to both the people and the process.

HELPFUL COMMUNICATION SKILLS

As noted previously, when you seek commitment from others, communications skills are a great help in stating and clarifying your concerns. A strong ability to communicate your concerns so that others hear *you* clearly seems self-evident. Similarly, you want to use all the skills you have to hear and understand *other people* as well.

Do you hear me?

Habermas (1981) pointed out that during verbal conflicts people may not agree because of one of four reasons. Either (1) they do not understand what was said; (2) they do not think other people meant what they said; (3) they do not think what was said is correct; or (4) they do not think it is appropriate for others to say what they said. Thus, when communicating your concern, clarity, sincerity, accuracy, and propriety are vital ingredients. The goal in communicating your concern is not simply to bring people to agreement. It also may provide a basis for a deeper understanding of the issues and the relationship.

Two of the most common behaviors mentioned in the literature regarding effective communication are *attending* and *listening*. Both of these behaviors are valuable when conferring as well as at higher levels of the Six-C Process.

Are you attending?

Attending seems simple enough, but with many relationships, especially during conflicts, it can be challenging to maintain consistent attention to what others are saying and doing. Attending relates to genuine eye contact, calm voice intonation, open posture, and other nonverbal behaviors that convey the message "I am with you," "I hear you," and "I understand you." To offer another person undivided attention is a powerful commitment, particularly in the midst of opposing perspectives. Genuine, undistracted attention is the underpinning for effective listening.

Are you listening?

Attending without listening is incomplete and risks violating trust in the relationship. Active listening is valuable because it exhibits your awareness and acceptance of people's opinions and feelings, a significant contribution to managing conflict in peaceful ways. Some of the behaviors that assist you in active listening when conferring about your concerns are *paraphrasing* and *reflecting,* two skills commonly used in professional counseling. Paraphrasing is the process of taking the *content* of what another person says and giving it back to the person, perhaps more succinctly, in different words to illustrate your understanding. Reflecting is the process of communicating to another person the *feeling* that you understand from what he or she has said. The following examples illustrate both paraphrasing and reflecting.

Paraphrasing

- **Example 1**

  Person says, "I am frustrated with all the tasks I have to accomplish at work."

  You paraphrase, "You have much to do in your job."

- **Example 2**

  Parent says, "I am at my wits end in dealing with this teenager of mine."

  You paraphrase, "Living with your teenager is proving to be quite challenging."

Reflecting

- **Example 1**

  Person says, "I am frustrated with all the tasks I have to accomplish at work."

  You reflect, "You seem overwhelmed with everything expected of you on the job."

- **Example 2**

  Parent says, "I am at my wits end in dealing with this teenager of mine."

  You reflect, "You are frustrated and maybe lost about how to relate to your teenager."

Each of these skills is useful in helping you convey understanding of both the content and feeling that a person has expressed. They demonstrate that you are attending and listening to what the other person is saying.

A lack of attending and listening is evident in the following episode.

A high school student got into a violent argument with his school counselor. He was being reprimanded and penalized for being late to school. He tried to explain that he had to stay home to meet the postman and get his mom's welfare check. Otherwise, his mother's boyfriend, a drug addict, would take it. The student's explanation seemed to fall on deaf ears. The student stormed out of the counselor's office complaining bitterly, "You won't even listen to me."

Often, conflicts persist because attempts at resolving them are unclear to everyone concerned. By being clear, seeking understanding, asking for feedback, and keeping channels open, you can create a stronger relationship in conferring about your concern.

A note about the importance of civility seems appropriate here. As you apply the strategies and tactics introduced in this book, keep in mind that civility, common courtesy, and politeness are signs of strength, not weakness. They bolster and enrich the dialogue you initiate with others when expressing your concerns. As noted by Kingsweel (1994), civility is much more than good manners and polite behaviors. Civility is the key to democratic interaction. It is the quality of being open to the perceptions of others coupled with an intentional monitoring of one's own perceptions. Civility may represent vigorous dissent, but always within a circle of respect for everyone involved.

All the communication skills mentioned in this and other chapters are useful to applying the Six-C Process successfully. They also function as an introduction to our specific formula for conferring that will help you assert yourself while maintaining a respectful posture. In this next section, we offer a simple but useful mnemonic formula for conferring.

THE 3+++WISH? FORMULA

Our formula for conferring is a practical application of communication skills. It looks like this: *3+++wish?* While simple in structure, the formula works in many, but not all, situations. It provides a straightforward pattern for communicating your concerns while avoiding potentially combative situations (see Illustration 3.1).

Illustration 3.1

The 3+++wish? Formula

3+++: Three positive signals that you come in peace

wish: Expressing exactly what it is you want

?: Ask that what you want will be given to you

The first part of the formula, 3+++ (three pluses), represents at least three indications that you are not here to fight. With each +, you signal a desire for a friendly and respectful encounter. These signals might be verbal (greeting, using the person's preferred name, choosing nonthreatening language, providing some small expression of pleasure or appreciation, etc.). The signals may also be nonverbal (tone and reflection of voice, eye contact, hand shake, smile, head nod, etc.). The purpose of each + is to signal to others in a respectful way that you come in peace to address a concern.

Before moving forward, we want to convey that the 3+++ can also signal the significance and value you give to the relationship with which you have a concern. Through these "plus comments," you communicate that mutual respect complements your committed stance—one that recognizes potential for growth and remains open to new information and possibilities.

Using the 3+++wish? formula works best in one-on-one situations with as much privacy as possible. Expressing a concern in front of others often leads to defensive posturing. The other party might see you as public grandstanding. Moreover, expressing a concern in public makes it difficult to change your stated positions. As Fisher, Ury, and Patton (1991) pointed out in their classic book, *Getting to Yes,* "No matter how many people are involved in a negotiation, important decisions are typically made when no more than two people are in the room" (p. 36; see also Ury, 1993). It is helpful to keep third parties out of the equation until their presence and input are necessary. As we will explain in Chapter 4, their presence is more helpful at a higher level of the Six-C Process.

Ideal democratic relationships might move us beyond this concern of public showboating; where we strive for public discourses in which people freely express feelings and thoughts and communicate openly without worry of defensive posturing or grandstanding. However, most conflict situations you experience today do not yet reflect this ideal.

We might expect that educators and other professionals who typically score well on emotional climate measures would consistently exhibit the 3+++ in showing respect for students and others. When speaking to students, educators who score well are in close proximity, establish eye contact before speaking, and address them by name. According to Pianta (2008), these professionals consistently have a warm and calm voice and use language that conveys respect, such as saying, "Please," "Thank you," and "You are welcome." The absence of harshness and tension is evident.

Individuals are much more sensitive to these + signals than they may seem. Mannerisms make a big difference in interpersonal relationships. This is illustrated by an experience described by Henry Ford, inventor of one of the earliest automobiles. The young Henry Ford had endured criticism and ridicule for his internal combustion engine. During that period, most experts were convinced that electric carriages were the wave of the future. One evening, Henry attended a dinner in which Thomas A. Edison was the guest of honor. During the meal, Henry began to explain his ideas to a group of people nearest to him at the table. The great Thomas Edison overheard Henry and moved closer. He asked Henry to make a drawing of his invention. When the crude sketch was completed, Edison considered the drawing, then suddenly banged his hand on the table. "Young man," he said, "That's the thing! You have it!" Years later, Henry Ford recalled, "The thump of that hand upon the table was worth worlds to me."

In addition to signaling positive intent, the +s also reduce uncertainty. Berger and Calabrese (1975) explored initial inter personal interactions. According to their uncertainty reduction theory, when strangers meet, they seek to reduce uncertainty about each other and their intent. Simultaneously, during this entry phrase of relationship development, people seek to increase their ability to predict their partner's and their own behavior in the situation. As uncertainty is reduced, verbal communication will increase. Moreover, increases in uncertainty produce decreases in liking, while decreases in uncertainty produce increases in liking. Thus, the initial contact is designed to be as positive as possible, as represented by the 3+++'s

The 3+++ is followed by a *wish*. The wish is a verbal request for assistance in handling a particular concern. In making the wish, it is important to choose your words carefully. The Six-C Process stresses the value of changing from negative to positive language. Here are some examples:

lost	becomes	misplaced
never	becomes	unlikely
impossible	becomes	difficult
if	becomes	provided
absolute	becomes	perhaps
must	becomes	want
need	becomes	prefer
never	becomes	rarely

always	becomes	often
problem	becomes	situation (or even *opportunity*)
but	becomes	and
no running	becomes	please walk
subordinate	becomes	associate
visitor	becomes	guest

A growing number of research studies have pointed out the beneficial effects of optimistic beliefs manifested in positive self-talk. Research by Scheier and Carver (1993), Seligman (1975, 2006), Purkey (2000), and others indicates that positive beliefs coupled with positive internal dialogue have beneficial results in most areas of human activity.

Using a language of optimism is not the same as the current political term *spin*, where political "spin doctors," twist facts to place opponents in the worst possible light, while flattering themselves. Spin is about distortion. By contrast, a language of optimism is genuine and trustworthy. We base the Six-C Process on the democratic principles of respect for people and their need for communicative authenticity.

The democratic principles advocated in this book also mean that in choosing your language carefully, you are attentive to the veracity of the wish you convey. Do you genuinely and honestly mean what you say? In addition, will your wish be mutually beneficial in fostering the relationship, or might it threaten the other person? If your wish potentially threatens the relationship, is the risk worth it? These questions encourage you to explore the trustworthiness of your stance. As a trait, trustworthiness relates so closely to respect that the two go hand in hand.

Trustworthiness is another term for personal and professional integrity. In his book, *The Integrity Dividend: Leading by the Power of Your Word*, Simons (2008) pointed out that besides being trustworthy for its own sake and because it is the right thing to do, being trustworthy brings dividends in many seemingly unrelated areas of living, both personally and professionally. It is often more productive to make a request that you know is based on mutual respect and democratic values.

The final step in the 3+++wish? is the willingness and courage to ask directly for what you want. Your request should be intentional and unmistakable. As a reminder, the surest way to get what you want is to ask for it. Forni (2008) advised that, whenever possible, you should exploit the remarkable power of asking for what you want. When making a wish, ask for what you want, as opposed to what you do not want. For example, "I wish you would turn off cell phones during this meeting" is more direct than "I wish you would not use your cell phones." Asking for something validates the power of the other party. Thus, the other person is less likely to become defensive or hostile. Moreover, by asking, you are enlisting his or her help in finding a solution to your concern.

Key Point 3.4

Having the courage to make a direct request is half the battle. This is often the most challenging and difficult step for many people.

In a nonthreatening, nonjudgmental way, you give three signals of good intent, state your request (wish), and ask that it be granted. Having the courage to make a direct request is half the battle. This is often the most challenging and difficult step. Sometimes, people shrink from communication with others to avoid potential unpleasantness. You have to ask for the order if you expect to get it.

The ultimate goal of the 3+++wish? formula is to reach a desirable end. According to the Harvard Negotiating Team (Fisher, Ury, & Patton, 1991), this is known as "getting to yes." The purpose is to obtain a positive response from the person receiving the request. Obtaining verbal commitment is your linchpin in determining the satisfactory results of your efforts.

As an illustration of lack of commitment and its negative effects, consider that many years ago financially strapped teachers sold encyclopedias to parents and others to supplement their meager salaries. The teachers did a wonderful job in describing the many advantages and beautiful features of the encyclopedias and demonstrating the merits of the books. Yet, they tended to be unsuccessful salespersons. The reason is that they could not bring themselves to ask the potential customer directly, "Will you buy these encyclopedias from me?" They could not ask for the order. By not asking for a commitment to buy the encyclopedias, the teachers avoided rejection. Their fear of failure prevented them from being successful salespersons.

Key Point 3.5

Obtaining verbal commitment is your linchpin in
determining the future success of your efforts.

Now that the structure of the 3+++wish? formula has been
introduced, here are seven examples of how the formula works in
everyday life both personally and professionally.

Example 1: A student uses inappropriate language in the hallway. The
teacher, using the 3+++wish? formula, stops the student in a friendly
manner, perhaps smiles, and says, "Mary, I would appreciate it if you used
proper language. Will you do this for me?" (Notice the 3+++wish?
formula embedded in the request.)

Example 2: A colleague borrows your computer flash drive without
asking permission to take it. You approach the colleague in a friendly
way, perhaps smile, and say, "John, I enjoy sharing this office with you.
And, I wish that you would ask me before taking my flash drive. Will you
do this for me?" Again, it is essential to ask directly for what you want. No
one can read your mind.

Example 3: A colleague is overly friendly with you. He has the tendency to
call female colleagues, "Sweetheart" (or, in the case of a female colleague,
she calls her male friends, "Stud"). For you, this is an actionable concern.
You approach your colleague in private, give several nonverbal cues (stance,
tone of voice, smile, etc.) that you are not looking for a confrontation, then
say something like, "We've worked in the same building for three years.
You've taught me a lot, and I appreciate your generosity. I do wish you
would call me by my proper name. Would you do this for me?"

Example 4: At a family gathering, a relative makes a racial slur. You
meet it with silence and a frown. Then you wait until you can be alone
with the relative. After several signals that you respect your relative and
wish no harm, you gently comment, "I have great fondness for you. You
are always the life of the party. And, I wish that you would show respect
for others by avoiding racial comments. Would you do this for me?"

Example 5: *Your teenage son or daughter comes home from band practice and drops his or her band instrument in the middle of the living room. In response, you give your child a hug, ask how the practice went, then say, "I'm glad you are home safe. And, would you please place your tuba in your room? Would you do this for me?"*

Example 6: *Imagine that you are a school principal. One of your teachers has the habit of leaving school often before all the students are out of the building. (You worry that he might trample some students in his haste to beat the buses.) Using the 3+++wish? formula, you visit his classroom, perhaps sincerely compliment on the room's appearance and arrangement, smile, and say, "You are having a good year, Charlie, and you are a great role model for our younger teachers. And, I do wish you would remain in the building until all the students have gone home. Would you do this for me?"*

Example 7: *Returning to the opening episode of this chapter, where the school custodian is caught having a smoking break on the edge of campus, you might try something like this: "Elma, I appreciate how well you keep this school clean. I know you take pride in your work. I do wish that you would please smoke off campus. Would you do this for me?"*

In each of the above examples, notice the use of *and* rather than *but*. Sometimes, well-intentioned people use the word *but*, not realizing that this word often signals a significantly negative message. For example, "I believe in racial equality, but . . ." Here, the word *but* signals that you can disregard everything I have said, because now I am going to tell you what I really believe. In this way, *but* not only signals a forthcoming negative remark, it also negates anything said previously.

From these seven examples, you can see the structure of the formula at work. Each one illustrates positive signals that demonstrate respect for yourself and the other person. Each contains a wish that you have clearly expressed. Finally, each contains a request for the person to behave a certain way or do something specifically.

We cannot emphasize enough the role that respect plays in formulating and expressing your concern in every situation. Chapter 1 mentioned several additional points to keep in mind when expressing a concern. These include an appreciation of the varied perceptions that people have of the same situation and the importance of clear communication to relay your concerns.

> *One of the authors was explaining the 3+++wish? formula to a group when a participant said that this approach was phony because people would know, "You are only saying something nice to them before you drop the bomb." When it was explained that the way to overcome this perception was to communicate positive and realistic comments to people at other times, the person said, "I don't know if I want to do that. But I will think about it."*

One way to avoid the appearance of being phony is to use the formula regularly. By integrating it into your daily interactions, it will become an authentic part of who you are.

To reiterate what we stated earlier, when you first express the 3+++ of a given relationship, it is essential that you state them authentically. It is unlikely that you will sustain a respectful and trustworthy relationship if your initial greetings, cordial recognitions, and openness to work collaboratively are less than sincere—or worse, disingenuous. Avoid platitudes and fraudulent compliments at all times. Be selective and sincere in the pluses you choose in beginning the conferring formula.

One final caveat is necessary; nothing works in the face of stupidity. The 3+++wish? formula is only useful when you use your own unique methods, skills, knowledge, and intelligence to make it work. The formula requires a certain art to make it look effortless. In fact, the apparently effortless is the hallmark of success. The formula should not call attention to itself. Making the 3+++wish? invisible is the hardest part of all. It requires intention and purpose coupled with respect and integrity. Try the practice session that follows. It provides a couple of situations and then gives you starter stems for each part of the 3+++wish?. In each exercise, complete the stems and read them back to yourself to check how they might sound to another person. Remember in each case that appropriate nonverbal body language is important. After you are satisfied with your responses to these scenarios, make up others more real to your life and work and try out the 3+++wish? formula.

PRACTICING THE 3+++WISH? FORMULA

1. *At work, all employees have assigned parking spaces. A colleague in the parking space next yours constantly straddles the line between spaces. This has been a problem for you in getting in and out of your car—not enough space and you worry about your door hitting the other car.*

   3+++: Good morning, _____ (colleague's name), I appreciate _____

   wish: And, I wish _____

   ?: Would you _____?

2. *You are a teacher meeting with a parent about a child's poor reading performance. In past meetings, the parent has promised to listen to the child read at least three times a week. Follow-up by you has discovered that the parent has not kept this promise.*

   3+++: Good afternoon, _____ (parent's name), I want to thank you _____

   wish: And, I wish _____

   ?: Would you ? _____?

3. *A friend is consistently late to social functions that you plan. In the past, you have made light of it, but it has now become an actionable concern.*

   3+++: Hello, _____ (friend's name), I always enjoy your company _____

   wish: And, I wish _____

   ?: Would you _____?

4. *A student frequently makes nonthreatening but inappropriate physical contact with other students (e.g., tickling, grabbing, hugging, nudging). Other students have complained to you about this student's behavior.*

   3+++: Thanks for staying after so we can talk. You are _____

   _____

   wish: And, I wish _____

   ?: Would you _____?

You might have guessed that, as practical as the 3+++wish? formula is, it is not fail safe. When conferring with another person, you may have to handle challenges that interfere with obtaining his or her commitment. Other times, people might overtly reject your wish. Each of these scenarios deserves special attention.

HANDLING CHALLENGES

When using the 3+++wish? formula, one challenge you may face is to limit discussion to one concern at a time. If the person or persons to whom you address your concern bring(s) up counterconcerns, explain that you will consider their concerns as soon as the present concern is addressed. It is vital to address one concern before introducing additional ones. If the other person brings up a secondary concern, explain that you will address additional concerns as soon as he or she helps you resolve the present concern.

> Suppose as a school counselor you confer with parents about their daughter's apparent sleepiness in school. It appears the girl is getting insufficient sleep at home. The parents respond by complaining about the rudeness of the school secretary. You express regret about the rudeness they experienced and assure them that you will look into the matter as soon as they help you address the initial concern about their daughter. You then quickly return to the daughter's falling asleep in class. "Mr. and Mrs. Smith, we appreciate you coming in for this conference. You have a fine daughter, and we both want her to take advantage of the educational opportunities offered at the school. A good night's rest will increase the likelihood of her academic success. We ask that you make sure she gets at least nine hours of sleep each night, which is the recommended amount of sleep for children her age. Will you do this for us?"

A second challenge in seeking commitment is to avoid taking detours that are often put in place in the form of questions regarding the *why* of a particular concern. The *why* of a concern should be held in reserve until absolutely unavoidable (in Chapter 4, we explain this further). The reason is that talking about *why* can easily become a time-consuming distraction that leads to endless regressions. To illustrate, a teacher might ask a student, "Why didn't you do your homework?" The student replies with a very long-winded tale, "My homework paper was used by my dad to line the canary cage, and canaries are very messy. One died last year, and we plan to buy a new one, but Dad is out of work so we live with Aunt Lizzie. She does not like birds, and so I don't know what we'll do . . ." and on and on—an endless response having nothing to do with the concern at hand.

In sum, it is best not to spend time and energy at this conferring level explaining *why* something is of concern. It bogs things down explaining to a student *why* walking in the hallway promotes the safety of everyone or explaining to an office mate *why* you want the stapler to remain on your desk, or telling to a colleague *why* you do not wish to be called by an overly familiar name. In conferring, it is best to avoid extended discussion of why some concerns are or are not accurate, fair, reasonable, or enforceable. Avoid the *why* of a concern until it is necessary to consider (at some higher Six-C level). All that is necessary at the conferring stage is to (1) signal good intentions, (2) make the wish, and (3) ask for the order.

HANDLING OUTRIGHT REJECTION

There will be times when your concern may appear to be of little or no concern to the other person. Your wish is denied. Nevertheless, as with the earlier example of the retired colleague who showed up for dinner illustrates, it sometimes takes a certain level of interpretation before deciding that the person is outright rejecting your request. Before assuming this, make sure that the other person has heard your request. Moreover, it may be necessary to negotiate a concern, such as a student coming late to class. Perhaps you and the person exhibiting the behavior (attitude, language, etc.) of concern could work out a solution to the benefit of everyone involved. (The music teacher might be willing to end her class on time so that students can reach their next classes without running in the halls.) When faced with obvious refusal to honor your wish, your choices are limited to aggression, acquiescence, or assertion (fight, flee, or simply stand your ground). We recommend the third choice.

There are two major situations when a concern is worth taking a stand over and moving to a higher level in the Six-C Process. The first is when the other person declines to be of assistance in resolving the concern. The second is when the other person agrees to be of assistance and then does not follow through. Each of these is worth a closer look.

When Cooperation Is Not Obtained

When faced with resistance, vary your approach. If the concern continues to be of significance, it may be possible to negotiate the matter. Negotiation is always a viable option. For example, if a student does not wish to participate in a particular exercise, the teacher might negotiate by asking, "What would you suggest to do in place of the exercise?" In the U.S. Navy, this is called "navigational mobility." Always have a way out in mind in case of emergencies. The willingness to be flexible goes hand in hand with assertiveness.

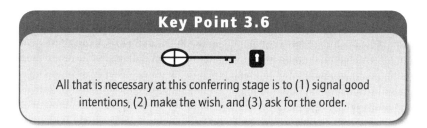

Key Point 3.6

All that is necessary at this conferring stage is to (1) signal good intentions, (2) make the wish, and (3) ask for the order.

When There Is No Follow-Through

We have all encountered people who promise to do something but do not live up to their word. Examples are everywhere. Repairmen who promise to be show up the next morning and don't, students who promise to keep their hands to themselves and don't, family members who give their word that they will turn the lights out when they leave a room and don't. When someone breaks his or her word and the situation is sufficiently important, it is time to continue the Six-C Process and move upward to the third level, *consult.*

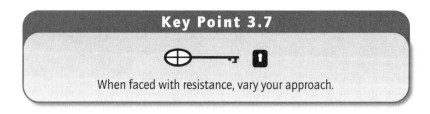

Key Point 3.7

When faced with resistance, vary your approach.

SUMMARY

Confer is the second C in the Six-C Process. This chapter introduced the basic qualities involved in conferring, focusing on disposition and behaviors to communicate clearly and respectfully. A mnemonic formula, introduced as *3+++wish?*, offered a simple but effective way of handling a concern at the lowest level while using the least amount of time and energy. We concluded this chapter with a series of explanations regarding challenges and rejection. The next chapter will consider the third C in the Six-C Process: *consult*.

Major Themes

- Conferring is the informal process of expressing your concern and asking for assistance in alleviating it with minimum time and energy spent by either you or the person with whom you have the concern. To confer with someone means to take action at a low level of interaction with as little investment and emotion as necessary.

- Although conferring is a low-level form of conflict resolution, it is helpful to use some cognitive structures that guide you to a satisfactory conclusion. The 3+++wish? formula presented in this chapter is a useful mnemonic escort that is simple in format (easy to remember) quick to apply (saves time and energy), and nonthreatening to other people in the process (maintains a high degree of respectfulness).

- Despite the simplicity and ease with which you confer with people about your concerns, the reality of many situations is that others might not view the concern the same way you do. Even if they do perceive the concern as you do, they may not make a commitment to help alleviate it or might attempt to distract you from the concern. More seriously, people might reject your request for assistance, refuse to cooperate, or fail to follow through on commitments they make. When these outcomes are evident, it is time to move to level 3, *consult*, which is a more structured and formal level of action.

CHAPTER FOUR

Consult

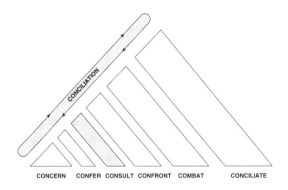

CONCERN   CONFER   CONSULT   CONFRONT   COMBAT   CONCILIATE

> *Your organization pays employees twice a month through direct deposit and sends nonnegotiable statements in the mail. Last pay cycle, you noticed errors on your statement and in checking your bank account found your pay was incorrect, less than it should have been! This was certainly an actionable concern and you immediately called the payroll office. Using the 3+++wish? formula, you pleasantly conferred with a representative in the payroll office. He assured you that the error would be corrected and the balance due you would appear in your next deposit statement. Two weeks have past and you received yet another incorrect statement. Now you are out additional pay because your concern has not been alleviated.*

When you have been less than successful in conferring about an actionable concern, it may be time to move upward to the next level of the Six-C Process: *consulting*. Consulting differs from conferring (when you informally express a concern) in that consulting reminds those involved of previous, yet unsuccessful, efforts to reach a desirable conclusion, and it is coupled with a formal, direct attempt to do so. In practice and by description, consulting may appear similar to conferring. As you consider this third level of the Six-C Process, consulting, the following ideas may help you to differentiate it from the second level, conferring. These ideas are the themes presented in this chapter.

- Consulting is a more structured, formal process than conferring. Consulting also is a discipline with theoretical foundations and research support.
- Consulting processes sometimes create a triangular structure in which the person of concern may be viewed separate from the situation. Conferring, on the other hand, does not necessarily create a structure or make this distinction.
- Consultations sometimes include other persons and experts who share information and knowledge that might help resolve a situation.

If your initial concern remains and ongoing assessment reveals that, if not addressed and resolved, further difficulties will ensue, it is appropriate to move to a higher level of intervention. At this third level, you construct a more formal and structured process than you needed in conferring. Such structure allows you to *consult* with the person or persons with whom you still have a concern.

By establishing a *consultation*, you signal to the other person or persons a desire to sustain the intended respectful relationship— teaching, counseling, befriending, loving, or other—while sending clear notice of how serious the situation is to you. Return to the vignette that opened this chapter and consider what additional formality or structure would help you move from *confer* to *consult* in getting your pay deposits straightened out. Here are a few suggestions that might give more structure. Review these, and add your own.

- Call the payroll representative, state the situation again, politely remind him or her that you were assured that the error was corrected, yet it still exists. Ask to schedule an appointment.

- At the appointed meeting, ask what procedures will be followed to correct the problem. Reapply the 3+++wish? formula to increase the chances that the next payroll deposit will be accurate.
- Before the meeting ends, ask what *you* could do to ensure the next deposit is accurate.

As you move from an informal process (conferring) to a more formal process (consulting), you will note distinctions between the two types of relationships. Some distinctions are obvious while others are subtle. Information in this section of the chapter will help to clarify these differences. Later sections of this chapter offer suggestions to consider when proceeding to the consulting level, a brief overview of professional consultation, and an example of a consulting sequence for you to use when moving to this higher level of the Six-C Process. This opening section presents a few ideas to consider and reflect on when you decide to consult about a concern.

CONSIDERING THE SITUATION

The decision to move from the conferring level to consulting rests with you because you are the person who initially expressed the concern. Usually, this is not a hasty decision; but in certain situations, such as when your paycheck is lower than it should be, immediate attention is appropriate. Especially in times of crisis, the luxury of extensive contemplation may not be an option for you. Rather, it will be time to take instant action.

Consider the following events, and ask yourself if they would allow time for you to consider delayed action, or if they require immediate consideration:

- A student in your class says, "I don't have my homework because my dad lost his job and we are living at the homeless shelter."
- A colleague with whom you have been conferring because he has been negligent about turning in monthly reports replies, "I do what is necessary for this job. There is no incentive for me to do more than that."
- Recently, you conferred with the local sheriff about increasing patrols in your neighborhood. Today, you saw suspicious activity at a house across the street.

- After conferring with parents about their child's behavior in school, you observe no positive change in the last month. You contact the parents again, and they say, "We are doing all we can do at home. He is your problem at school."
- A primary grade student with whom you have been conferring about rambunctious behavior on the playground has fallen off the jungle gym and has hit her head very hard.

In most cases when time is not critical, you are in a better position to reflect on important factors before moving to a higher level of action. Consider these eight behaviors when reflecting whether to consult about your concern:

1. Clarifying and monitoring your feelings

2. Sending I-messages

3. Reviewing expectations

4. Ensuring understanding

5. Emphasizing commitment

6. Considering reconceptualization

7. Reflecting on consequences

8. Assessing time available

Behavior 1: Clarifying and Monitoring

Clarifying and monitoring your feelings about the situation may be important as you move to a next level of the Six-C Process. By examining your feelings about the situation, you might answer this question: "Why do I have this concern?"

Key Point 4.1

The decision to move from the conferring level to consulting rests with you, the person who initially expressed the concern.

Clarifying and monitoring your feelings might also be productive in two additional ways. First, you may see that the concern is more personal than you realize. Ask yourself, "Is there something in my background or behavior that is making this situation to be more of a concern than it needs to be?" "Could it be that the other person's position is justified?" If your answers to these questions are yes, you might be more productive in handling the concern through personal exploration than through consultation with others. Second, by becoming more aware of your feelings about the concern, you may be more able to keep your emotions in check as the consultation proceeds.

Think about the following feeling statements:

- I feel threatened by the words and actions this person uses.
- My heartbeat increases when I am in this situation.
- I can feel myself getting anxious when I am conferring with this person.
- This concern is no longer a minor inconvenience; I get angry when I think about it.

How might similar statements and questions help you understand why you have a particular concern? Feeling statements can help you assess the reasons behind the attention you give to any situation. These reasons constitute the underlying dynamics of your concern; and by exploring the underlying dynamics, you can better maintain a healthy and balanced perspective of various situations. By using a balanced approach, you are able to recognize and express legitimate concerns and make rationale decisions about moving from the conferring to consulting processes.

A caution seems appropriate here. Sometimes, the reasons *why* you have a concern emanate from faulty thinking. For example, you might base your reasoning on "right or wrong" thinking. Imagine a teacher who assumes that there is only one answer or one way to look at things. This teacher lives in an all-or-nothing world where there is no middle ground, no gray areas. He or she believes that mistakes are clear evidence of inadequacy.

Chapter 2 explored some thoughts about *why* something is of concern to you. Now that you have reached the consulting level of the Six-C Process, it seems sensible and appropriate to explain to the other person *why* something is a concern. In offering this explanation, focus on the concern itself and not on the person or individuals involved. One way to ensure that you do this is to be certain of the words you use to explain the reason for your concern. An approach called *I-messages* may be helpful in achieving this goal.

Behavior 2: Sending I-messages

Sending I-messages is a way to take responsibility for your feelings. Some theorists have offered I-messages as a way of conveying feelings of concern (Gordon, 2000; Ury, 1993). Using this approach, you present the concern, explain your feelings about *why* you have this concern, and describe its effects on *you*. When using I-messages, you replace the word *you* with the word *I*. Here are two examples:

> A teacher says to a student, "You were not paying attention." Instead, the same teacher might say, "I want to help you listen so I can be confident that you are learning the material."
>
> A principal says to a student referred for discipline, "You had better watch your mouth, buster!" Instead, the same principal says, "I only need to hear helpful language. Otherwise, I will have difficulty helping you with this problem."

For another illustration, compare the different approaches of two parents:

> The first parent might express a concern to a child by saying, "You left dirty dishes in the sink, and that makes me angry!" The second parent, using I-messages, expresses it differently stating, "I feel that you don't care when dirty dishes are in the sink, and I have to do extra cleanup. I become angry."

From all the above examples, you can see how I-messages demonstrate ownership of your feelings and how you connect those feelings to the actions of another person. I-messages express the reality that another person's behavior does not *make* you angry. Rather, you *choose* to be angry at the behavior you observe.

The statements that follow give you more illustrations of I-messages. Use these examples to construct your own responses to real situations in your personal and professional life.

- When students do not pay attention, I feel incompetent as a teacher.
- When I am left out of group, I feel rejected.
- I get angry when my supervisor makes suggestive remarks.
- I am scared when you don't come home on time.
- I feel hurt and humiliated when anyone corrects me in public.

Once you achieve a balanced perspective of a situation and understand the underlying emotional dynamics of I-messages, you may find it is easier to decide whether or not to proceed to the consultative level. If you think it is appropriate to continue, review your expectations of what might happen as you move forward.

Behavior 3: Reviewing Expectations

Reviewing expectations is a way of reflecting on what you hope to accomplish. At times, it is appropriate for you, who owns the concern, to step back and think about the expectations you have had from the beginning of the situation. Bringing those expectations back into focus may help to determine the feasibility, practicality, and appropriateness of continuing with the issue. During such reflection, it is best to focus on a single problem rather than a number of issues. Equally important, you will want to pay attention to the situation rather than an individual or group of people involved in your concern.

Suppose you are a teacher who is concerned about the distraction caused by students packing up their books before class has ended. You have conferred with the students about your concern (using the 3+++wish? formula), but that did not produce a desirable outcome. Surreptitiously, they continue to pack up. Upon reflection, you decide that this is a normal and understandable student behavior (remember when you were a student?). Rather than focusing on students' packing up of books, you choose to focus on ways that you can orderly end each class.

When you doubt the significance of your original concern, it is worth weighing such doubt against the time and effort needed to move to a higher level of action. Too often, bothersome situations continue because they take on a life of their own. People want to save face, or other agendas subvert the original intent. Taking time to reconsider your initial observations and reflecting on their importance when measured against other pressing issues might be prudent steps to take.

Key Point 4.2

When you doubt the significance of the original concern, it is worth weighing such doubt against the time and effort needed to move to a higher level of action.

Behavior 4: Ensuring Understanding

Ensuring understanding is an ongoing part of the Six-C Process and is particularly helpful as you move to a higher level of action. If you decide the situation continues to be worth pursuing, the next consideration is whether the other individual fully understands the scope of the matter. One idea is to ask the other person to explain the situation from his or her point of view. This helps to ensure that each party understands what the other person has said. Without such understanding by the other person, it is difficult for you to raise the discourse to a higher level. Consequently, it is difficult to move to a consultation about a situation.

Key Point 4.3

Ask the other person to explain your concern from his or her point of view. This helps to ensure that each party understands what the other person has said.

To move a consulting relationship forward and attain a level of understanding, you want to maintain genuine communication, keep emotions in check (be cool), use humor when appropriate, and leave options open to everyone. Here, it is appropriate to emphasize the original commitments made by all parties in the process. It is also appropriate to consider compromise and/or reconceptualization in resolving your concern.

> *One of the authors and his spouse have developed a numerical way of ensuring understanding and communicating the significance of a concern. For example, using a 10-point scale, one partner evaluates the concern as a 7 in importance, while the other ranks it as only a 3. The partner who ranks the concern with the lower number understands the significance of the issue to the other.*

Behavior 5: Emphasizing Commitment

Emphasizing commitment returns you to an important action described in Chapter 3. Once people have given their word that they will help to reach a satisfactory conclusion to the original concern, it is difficult to recant (e.g., "Yes, I will ask before taking the stapler"; "Yes, I will smoke off schools grounds"; "Yes, I will walk in the school hallway"; "Yes, I will call you by the name you prefer"; "Yes, I will be home by midnight"; "Yes, I will clean up after my dog").

Giving your word about doing something means that if you fail to do it, you run the risk of others viewing you as unreliable, dishonest, or worse. Moreover, you are likely to experience dissonance. Very few people want to think of themselves as untruthful or be considered such by others. Thus, a critical step in resolving a situation through consultation is to remind others of their commitment (e.g., "You told me that you would remove the cardboard blocking the window in your classroom door. Your word is important to me. Would you please remove the cardboard?"). Even at the third level, *consult*, you continue to follow the basic principles of the Six-C Process and the *3+++wish?* formula described in Chapter 3. Reminding others of their verbal obligation is often a highly successful tactic in resolving frustrating concerns.

Behavior 6: Considering Reconceptualization

Considering reconceptualization is something you do before and after you clarify expectations, confirm understanding of all involved, and obtain their commitment. The type of reconceptualization that you might experience here involves questions such as

- Is there a compromise that would be acceptable and beneficial to everyone involved?
- Might there be another perspective that I could take about this concern and that would lessen its importance?

Because perceptions play such a significant role in determining the importance of particular concerns, reconceptualization is a valuable tool to use throughout the Six-C Process. Sometimes, by reframing a concern, you lessen its importance in the overall scheme of things. An example of reconceptualizing a concern might be helpful here.

A high school football coach and the school band director were having an increasingly angry argument over a multitalented student who was both an all-state musician and an outstanding athlete. The coach and the director both wanted the student's time for practice after school. Informal conferring between the two educators did not produce results. The school counselor stepped in and suggested that they reframe their concerns to reflect what was best for the student. In doing so, the coach and band director asked the student for his opinion. The student responded by inquiring if it was possible to be both an athlete and musician. Through this dialogue, the coach, band director, and student decided that the concerns should now be "How do we structure practices and performances to accommodate the student?" Consequently, they agreed to divide time for after-school practice between the two activities. In addition, the student played on the football team in the first quarter and most of the second quarter during games. He also performed with the band at halftime. After the half-time performance, the student was able to rejoin the team for the second half. Everyone was happy with the new arrangement, especially the student, who was no longer caught in the crossfire.

Behavior 7: Reflecting on Consequences

Considering the consequences of doing nothing is a reflection that may follow reconceptualization of a concern. If you conclude that a problem is no longer an important issue, the consequences of doing nothing may still need your attention. What might have happened in the above example of the musician-athlete if neither the coach nor the band director took the counselor's advice?

As another example, suppose a school custodian notices an emergency exit blocked by a shipment of textbooks, but because other tasks are on his schedule, he does nothing to report it or remove the boxes. His decision that other priorities should prevail might have tragic consequences. Violation of safety and fire regulations requires immediate action. When you decide, "This issue is no concern," give some attention to what might happen next.

Sometimes, your decision to put aside a concern may affect other people who were not part of the original problem. Here is an example:

A teacher had the habit of arriving a few minutes late to school most mornings. The principal knew that the teacher was a single parent who had to get two small children ready for day care and drop them off before coming to school. Because of these demands, the principal did nothing about the teacher's tardiness. Recognizing the slack policy, other teachers began arriving late to school. The result was that the principal had to accelerate from initial concern higher up the Six-C Process, to confront, in addressing the growing habit of faculty members being tardy to work.

Enabling some people to avoid their responsibilities, even when seemingly good reasons are apparent, can cause serious consequences for everyone involved. Therefore, take a broad view of the situation when you ignore a concern or defer action. Anticipate what the consequences might be for the larger audience.

Behavior 8: Assessing Time Available

Assessing the time available helps you to decide how much time to spend reflecting on your concerns. Ingredients to look for in determining whether time is available are factors such as safety issues, schedules, deadlines, or other circumstances that will limit the time needed for reflection. When time is not a factor, reflection takes its course, and your decision to move more slowly toward a higher level of action is appropriate.

In moving to the consult level of the Six-C Process, you will benefit from having some knowledge and understanding of consulting relationships. The next section offers a brief summary of types of consultation and structures useful in establishing a consult when addressing a concern. Understanding the basic structure of consulting relationships will help you to distinguish it from the previous level of conferring.

WHAT IS A CONSULTING RELATIONSHIP?

In many professions, consultation has become a distinct discipline with theoretical underpinnings and research findings (Brown, Pryzwansky, & Schulte, 2006; Dougherty, 2009; Parsons & Kahn, 2005; Schmidt, 2008). Within this discipline, three basic forms of consultation exist. They are (1) *informational*, (2) *instructional*, and (3) *problem solving*. A word about each might be helpful.

Informational consultation, as its name implies, consists of interventions that provide material, resources, and other content to convey information to an individual or audience. As an example, a community representative who speaks to a group of parents and children about summer camps and other recreational programs after school or during summer break is acting as a consultant who provides information.

Instructional consultation is similar to informational consultation. One difference is that instruction imparts more than simply information. Through instructional consultation, participants acquire knowledge and skills, learning new ways of approaching various situations. A nurse who instructs a patient on using a syringe to self-inoculate is an example of instructional consultation.

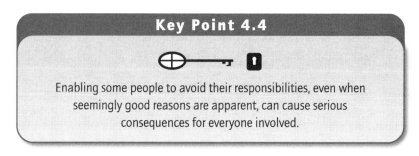

Key Point 4.4

Enabling some people to avoid their responsibilities, even when seemingly good reasons are apparent, can cause serious consequences for everyone involved.

Problem-solving consultation is most likely to be the type of consulting to choose in addressing difficult situations that have not responded to your use of conferring to address an actionable concern. The remainder of this chapter highlights a problem-solving mode of consultation as a basic approach to use at the third level of the Six-C Process. Providing information and giving instruction may be incorporated when appropriate, but in general, problem-solving consultation uses a triangular structure to address concerns and arrive at mutually beneficial decisions (Parsons & Kahn, 2005; Schmidt, 2008).

USING A TRIANGULAR STRUCTURE

A triangular view of consultation helps you to differentiate this level of action from the conferring level. This view attempts to separate the person receiving your consultation from the situation with which you have concern. Unlike conferring, which may view the person and the concern as a single issue, consulting begins by creating a psychological distance between the person of concern and the concern itself. An example to distinguish this subtle difference might be helpful.

A student is not completing or turning in homework assignments. At the conferring level, where you view the student and lack of homework as a single issue, you might offer suggestions to the student that could enable him or her to attack the homework problem. In dealing with this same issue at the consulting level, where you view the student and homework as separate entities, you and the student might explore barriers or obstacles that are unique to his or her homework situation.

Key Point 4.5

Unlike conferring, which may view the person and the concern as a single issue, consulting begins by creating a psychological distance between the person of concern and the concern itself.

Diagram 4.1 illustrates this triangular structure. The illustration depicts a person with a concern (e.g., a teacher), a person of concern (e.g., a student), and the concern (e.g., lack of completed homework assignments). In this instance, you, the teacher, establish an egalitarian relationship with the student (the person of concern) to examine ways that he or she can address, manage, or otherwise resolve the situation (incomplete homework assignments) in the best interest of all parties.

Diagram 4.1   Triangular Structure for Consultation

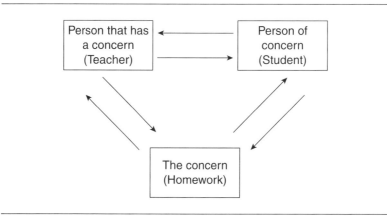

Emphasis on an egalitarian relationship is important because it resonates with the democratic ideal introduced in Chapter 1. As a related matter, it is also important to emphasize that within this type of consultation, *voluntary compliance* is essential. We believe it is unlikely that you can coerce people—students, parents, or others—into a meaningful and beneficial consultation.

Regardless of the relative status held by each person outside of a consultation, *within* the consulting process, the value and importance that each person brings to the process is paramount to its success. Returning to the illustration of Diagram 4.1, if a classroom teacher is consulting with a student about incomplete course assignments, they both bring valuable perspectives and expertise to the table. The teacher is the expert educator who understands the necessity of completing course assignments in making academic progress. At the same time, the student is the expert about himself or herself, the family life, and other factors that may be contributing to the concern. Both perspectives have value in trying to address the concern and move forward with a decision and commitment.

In a triangular consultation, the ultimate goal is to find a solution that is mutually beneficial to both parties. In doing so, the triangular structure keeps the problematic situation external to the relationship. In the example of the teacher and student, the triangular structure allows them to maintain a healthy working relationship in the classroom while exploring ways that the student could use to complete course assignments on time. In the end, the student has primary responsibility for completing the assignments. The teacher's responsibility is to help the student find ways to accomplish that goal.

Sometimes, simple triangular associations do not result in a successful conclusion. When that happens, you (the consultant) might seek assistance from others and alter the configuration of the consultation.

INVOLVING OTHERS IN A CONSULTATION

With any conflict, it is possible that neither you—the consultant—nor the other person has all the expertise or answers. When that is the case, you may want to involve other people. Usually, the decision of whether or not to do so is your prerogative. (Remember, you are the consultant who owns the concern.) But either party can initiate interest in bringing others into the consultation.

When you include other people in a consultation, it is usually because they bring some expertise, knowledge, sensitivity, or other information that may be useful in mediating the conflict. Involving others is a central ingredient in *conciliation,* which we explain in Chapter 7.

The possibilities may seem limitless of the people to involve, but it is important that those you include understand the reason why they are involved and the role they will play in the consultation. The rationale for including other people and the role they will play is essential for you to clarify. Such clarification helps you explain the nature of the original concern, focus on its importance, and avoid dealing with unessential information or unnecessary strategies. At all times, you maintain an assertive role in the process because the concern is yours.

Key Point 4.6

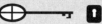

When you include other people in the consultation, it is usually because they bring some expertise, knowledge, or other information that may be useful in mediating the concern.

By returning to the example of the teacher consulting with the student about incomplete course assignments, we can apply the notion of additional consultants. Perhaps the teacher and student might want to include parents or guardians in the consultation. Such involvement could help the teacher understand the student's home life more fully and at the same time allow the student and parents to explore the concern in the context of their lives. All parties might arrive at solutions that would help the student complete assignments. In addition, mediation, arbitration, and even adjudication, though not the primary focus of this book, can assist in resolving concerns. The following story provides another example of including other consultants. It is a case where one of the authors was supervising a school counselor.

The school counselor was frustrated with a fourth-grade boy who was frequently being disruptive in the cafeteria. The student would get upset with his lunch and start tossing food at other students. Despite the counselor's efforts with individual and group counseling, success in helping the student resolve this problem was lacking. After the supervisor met with the counselor, he asked to meet with the classroom teacher and cafeteria manager. The first question asked in this meeting was, "What is the process for getting lunch in the cafeteria?" The teacher and cafeteria manager explained how students went through the line and selected different food based on what the staff was serving that day: "Peas or carrots?" "Ham or turkey?" "Potatoes or rice?" The teacher observed that for the student in question these decisions were particularly difficult. Sometimes, the cafeteria staff would get impatient and simply state, "If you cannot decide, then I will give you..." This usually infuriated the student and these would be the instances when he would sit at the table pouting and begin throwing food at other students.

Hearing this observation, the supervisor asked if the student could have his own copy of the school menu each morning. With his own copy, the student could select the items he wanted for lunch well before it was time to go to the cafeteria. After some discussion, the teacher and cafeteria manager agreed that the strategy had merit. The next day, the boy began receiving his own menu. After three weeks without an incident in the cafeteria, he told the teacher, "I don't need my own menu anymore. I can make my decisions in line with the other students."

The previous sections give a brief overview of consultation as a professional discipline. By necessity, they are brief, so you might want to explore references in this chapter to learn further detail. Successful consultation relies on a framework or structure to process information, data, perceptions, commitment, and other ingredients. The next section offers an example of one such framework for consulting.

SEQUENTIAL STEPS FOR CONSULTING

One of the authors has presented a model for problem-solving consultation called The Six Magic Steps of Consulting (Schmidt, 2004; Schmidt & Medl, 1983). Here, we adapt that model to use as a structure when moving through the consulting level in the Six-C Process. This adaptation includes six sequential steps to help you create a structure when consulting about a problem situation:

1. Identifying and confirming the relationship

2. Gathering pertinent data and information

3. Clarifying issues and understanding roles

4. Exploring options and strategies

5. Arriving at a decision and commitment

6. Evaluating and making rounds

Step 1: Identifying and Confirming the Relationship

Identifying and confirming the relationship are important to the first step of a problem-solving consultation. In the consulting level of the Six-C Process, appreciating a relationship and confirming its significance allow your concern to become genuine and transparent. You recognize the potential impact the situation may have on your association with the other person. An unresolved conflict jeopardizes all types of relationships and associations.

Whenever you express a concern, it usually involves another person or persons with whom you already have a connection and association. Such relationships cover a wide range of possibilities including friendships, family relations, work associations, teaching-learning partnerships, and countless others, including people you do not know. When conflicts remain unresolved in these myriad relationships, the personal and professional loss to you and others is immeasurable.

Even with strangers, you may have certain connections because you share space and time in given situations or at particular locations. For example, you might observe a stranger who breaks the line of patrons who are waiting for a table at a popular restaurant. Similarly, you could observe that a customer in the "Speedy Checkout" line has more than "20 Items or Fewer" in the grocery cart. If you decide these are actionable concerns, the principles of the Six-C Process might apply. Although observations such as these are commonplace, the vast majority of actionable concerns will be with people you know, such as relatives, friends, colleagues, and coworkers.

Confirming a relationship is a two-sided process. It takes both sides to agree that a connection exists and it is worth continuing. Without agreement on this point, it is difficult to imagine why either person or party would feel the same level of concern about a particular situation. Whether the concern involves a parent–child, teacher–student, supervisor–employee, counselor–client, stranger-to-stranger, or other type of association, the key to moving forward is for both sides to have an interest in maintaining a beneficial association. Once you and the other person have confirmed the value of the relationship, it is important to make a decision about whether or not to continue with the consult level.

It is possible that returning to the previous C—confer—may be all you need to do, and the formality of a consultation would be unnecessary. If, however, you see value in providing more structure to handle the conflict, then you can move to the next step of the sequence in consulting, gathering information.

Step 2: Gathering Pertinent Data and Information

Gathering pertinent data and information is essential in all problem-solving forms of consultation. You gather information from a variety of sources, including interviews, observations, surveys, and other sources of data (test scores, inventory profiles, etc.). When you have appropriate and accurate information, you are better able to invite people to rethink, reexamine, and reconceptualize concerns. If, on the other hand, you overlook essential data and pertinent information, you might rely on foolish notions, faulty beliefs, fantasy thinking, and mistaken conclusions—none of which is helpful in addressing concerns and resolving conflicts.

An example of a mistaken conclusion would be to enter a waiting area of a crowded airport and spot a passenger whose luggage is on a second seat. You think to yourself, "How rude." At that moment, a companion returns from the nearby water fountain, moves the luggage, and takes the seat next to the other passenger. Snap judgments can be faulty.

Once the gathering of information is complete and you have shared, reviewed, and discussed all that is appropriate with the other person, the next step is to gain clarity about the concern and the role each of you will play in resolving it. This part of the sequence, clarifying issues and roles, is often the most helpful in moving a consultation forward to a desired goal.

Step 3: Clarifying Issues and Understanding Roles

Clarifying issues and understanding roles means that you explain the problem and related issues once again. It may seem repetitious to do so, but by restating your concern at this time, you and all involved are able to affirm an understanding of the situation. Consequently, everyone is in a stronger position to examine alternatives and move toward a mutually beneficial resolution.

Ideally, each participant in a consultation assumes a specific role and accepts responsibility for that role. For example, in the case presented earlier between the teacher and the student with incomplete course assignments, the roles are clear. The teacher is responsible for helping the student learn course content, and therefore, the teacher provides appropriate assignments to reinforce such learning. The student is responsible for completing the assignments in a timely manner. Of course, this is the ideal situation. What happens if the teacher or student does not accept the designated role and respective responsibilities?

When you fail to perform expected responsibilities, your consultation loses steam and integrity. Similarly, when the other person in a consultation does not accept responsibility for his or her role, your likelihood of progressing toward a desired outcome decreases. In such a case, the fourth C in the Six-C Process—confront—may be called for. At the same time, when you assume responsibilities that rightfully belong to another person in the consultation, you weaken the chances of being successful. For example, if a teacher or a parent assumes responsibility for a student's assignments, they demonstrate disrespect toward the student and do a disservice to the child's development of responsibility. For this reason, it is important that you and others in a consultation *clarify* and *accept* designated roles and inherent responsibilities related to resolving the concern. Once everyone reaches clarification, you are ready to explore options and strategies to handle the situation.

Step 4: Exploring Options and Strategies

Exploring options and strategies to alleviate the problem is the fourth step of consultation as described here. This could include brainstorming a list of possibilities, examining strategies already attempted, and searching for resources that might provide additional ideas. For example, in talking with an elementary student who pushed another student, a principal might ask the aggressive student, "What could you have done that would have been more helpful?" This type of questioning might lead the student to explore more positive, nonaggressive behavior.

The goal in this stage of the sequence is to narrow the number of options and strategies to ones that have the most potential in resolving the conflict to the satisfaction of everyone involved.

Once you have achieved a reasonable list, the consultation moves toward a decision about which strategy or option to implement.

Step 5: Arriving at a Decision and Commitment

Arriving at a decision and commitment is a summation of all the prior steps in this sequence. At times, people consult about concerns and believe they have found workable solutions without ever making a clear decision and without gaining commitment to apply selected strategies. If that happens, you may find that the situation continues and sometimes festers, resulting in broken or damaged relationships. Consider the following scenario:

> A group of teachers asked the school counselor to facilitate a difficult conference with parents of an underperforming child. At the meeting, the counselor asked for ideas from the parents and the teachers, and they mentioned many possibilities. When the conference ended, however, participants accepted no assignments and made no commitments to work on the situation. The parents drove home thinking, "That went well. The counselor and teachers should be able to help our child and we will not have to worry about it any more." Collectively, the teachers thought, "Well, that will help. The parents will take charge of their child now, and the counselor will make sure the student performs better in class." Satisfied with the conference, the counselor went back to the office and patted himself on the back for a job well done. A month later, the teachers were angry with the parents and the counselor, and the parents, fed up with the situation, began home schooling their child.

As this story suggests, it is crucial that you diligently process this step of consultation—make a clear decision and get commitment from everyone to follow through with responsibilities. If you do not accomplish this, it may be necessary to return to step three—clarifying issues and roles—and reaffirm agreements everyone made previously or forge new agreements.

After decisions and commitments are clear and understood, you are able to implement strategies to address the conflict. Evaluative processes follow such implementation, which moves you to the final leg of this consultation sequence.

Step 6: Evaluating and Making Rounds

Evaluating and making rounds is the last step of this approach to consultation, and if you accomplish it, you will conclude most consultations satisfactorily. Please excuse us for repeating this like a mantra, but because you *own the concern,* you have primary responsibility to determine the progress made toward resolving it.

Key Point 4.7

When any participants in a consultation have not carried out commitments they made, it may be necessary to return to step three—clarifying issues and roles—and reaffirm agreements everyone made previously, or forge new agreements.

Similar to the second step of gathering data and information, evaluation takes countless forms from simple interviews and observations to more sophisticated processes such as structured questionnaires, formal testing, or third-party assessment. Whatever evaluation processes you choose, share results with everyone involved in the consultation. In that regard, you "make the rounds" by contacting everyone involved, checking on each person's implementation of responsibilities, and assessing the level of success in alleviating the problem.

Return to the story above about the school counselor facilitating the difficult parent conference. If you were the counselor, what strategies could you implement as part of the evaluation of the conference? Here are some starter ideas:

- Before ending the conference, ask participants for one specific behavior that they will use to help the student with school performance.
- After a week, visit each teacher and ask if he or she has used the specific behavior mentioned at the conference and what results have occurred.
- Send a handwritten note to the parents the day after the conference thanking them for their support. Restate the behavior they mentioned they would use to help their child.

- Call the parents after two weeks and ask them how they are making out with their new behavior. What changes, if any, have they observed?
- Talk with the student and ask if anything new has happened in class or at home.

There are limitless strategies to evaluate a consultation. Ultimately, you determine if the consultation has achieved its goal. That ultimate determination likely hinges on your feelings about the situation. If a consult does not produce an acceptable outcome and your initial concern persists, it may be time to consider a higher level of action.

Now that you have been introduced to the sequential steps of one approach to problem-solving consultation, it might be a good idea to practice it. Use the vignette that follows, and then attempt to answer questions in each of the steps.

Key Point 4.8

Whatever evaluation processes you choose, share results with everyone involved in the consultation. Ultimately, you determine if the consultation has achieved its goal.

PRACTICING THE CONSULTING SEQUENCE

You are the principal of an elementary school and one of your veteran teachers has been struggling with her fourth-grade class. Her class management is not up to the high standard it was in years past. Students are disruptive, the teacher has been shouting at them to calm down, the class has been disturbing other classrooms, and student achievement has not met expectations. You have conferred with the teacher, but the concern continues. Now, the situation requires a more formal approach.

Identifying and Confirming the Relationship

How would you begin to identify and confirm the relationship you have with this teacher?

Would you meet with her alone, or would you include others?

Where would you meet and why would you choose this location?

Would reflection on her past years as a teacher be helpful to you and to her?

What else would you want to accomplish in this first step of consultation?

Gathering Information

What types of data or information would be important to gather?

How would you get this information?

How would you share it with the teacher?

What information (or expertise) does the teacher have that might be helpful in this process?

Clarifying Issues and Understanding Roles

What are the dominant issues that make up your major concern?

What concerns might the teacher have that are relevant to the situation?

What is your role and what is the teacher's role in moving toward a resolution of these concerns?

Exploring Options

How would you proceed in exploring options and strategies?

Are there resources (e.g., other teachers) that might provide ideas for strategies?

How would you and the teacher narrow down potential strategies?

Arriving at a Decision and Commitment

When you and the teacher have narrowed down the options, how would you arrive at a decision?

What kind of commitment would you expect from the teacher?

What commitment would you make in moving the process forward?

What would you do if the teacher could not make a firm commitment to use one or more options?

Evaluating and Making the Rounds

As the teacher's supervisor, what would you do to assess the progress she is making with classroom management?

What type of evidence would you look for to ascertain whether your concern has been alleviated?

What would you do if the teacher has used the strategies, but her classroom management, student behavior, and student achievement remain unchanged?

What would you do if the teacher has not followed through with the strategies selected during the consultation?

When you have exhausted all your ideas and options at the consultation level without success, it is possible that you need to move to the next higher level in the Six-C Process. At this subsequent level, you *confront* the situation directly. Chapter 5 will explain confrontation as the next logical step in reaching a desirable outcome.

SUMMARY

In this fourth chapter, we considered the third level of the Six-C Process—*consult*—for expressing a concern and addressing a conflict. The chapter identified areas of reflection that may help you in determining whether to continue with your concern by moving to a more structured approach with the person or persons involved. A brief description and definition of *consultation* provided information about different types of consulting processes.

This chapter suggested that problem-solving forms of consultation might be appropriate when dealing with conflict. A sequence for problem-solving consultation offered a structure within which you could ask for commitment, clarify roles and responsibilities, process information and data, and evaluate outcomes.

When consultation has not resulted in a desired outcome, and your original concern persists, it may be time to move to the next level. At this point, the Six-C Process encourages you to *confront* the person or persons of concern and present the consequences that will occur if the situation is not resolved.

Major Themes

- Consulting is a more structured and formal process than is conferring, but the 3+++wish? formula continues to be useful in this and other levels of the Six-C Process.
- By reflecting on particular aspects of your feelings and expectations, understandings about a concern, commitment received from others, reconceptualization about the concern, the time available to handle the situation, and the prospect of doing nothing, you are in a stronger position when moving to the consult level of the Six-C Process.
- Consultation about a concern is best viewed as a problem-solving relationship. A sequential process of specific steps serves as a cognitive structure by which you can gather pertinent information, explore options, ask for commitment, evaluate outcomes, and reach a satisfactory conclusion.

CHAPTER FIVE

Confront

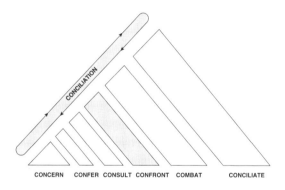

CONCERN   CONFER CONSULT CONFRONT COMBAT   CONCILIATE

As a university class was beginning, an older student slipped and fell heavily to the floor. Two younger students rushed to his aid and began to lift him. The professor advised the students against moving the fallen man in case he had suffered a serious injury, but the students were so excited they did not respond to the professor's concern. If you were the professor, what would you do?

We derive the term *confront* from the Latin word *confrontare*, which means to face and to challenge. Moving from consultation to confrontation is not a step you should take lightly. Usually, the first three levels of the Six-C Process (concern, confer, and consult) are the most you will need in finding a successful solution.

At times, however, you may have a concern that is not resolved by using lower levels, or you may not have time to do so. These are extreme challenges, which require you to immediately speed through or even leapfrog over lower levels and use direct, unwavering, and face-to-face confrontation. In the opening vignette, the professor faced a situation where students ignored his warning not to move their fallen classmate. When his advice went unheeded, the professor took immediate action and confronted the situation.

The professor instantly moved up the process to a higher C level and confronted the students with a demand: "Do not move him!" The students heard the command and stopped lifting the man. When the emergency rescue squad arrived, the medics quickly determined that the man had indeed suffered a serious injury. The medics said that had the students lifted him, they could have done more damage. Sometimes, quick and forceful confrontation is unavoidable and entirely appropriate.

This chapter presents the level at which you decide to confront a situation because previous levels have not produced desired results. Please keep in mind that you are confronting a situation, not a person. This chapter offers ideas and questions to ask as you begin to confront. A large part of this chapter is devoted to exploring the idea of "constructive confrontation" found in current literature (Burgess & Burgess, 1996, 1997; Hoover & DiSilvestro, 2005). This chapter concludes with a few practical ideas for you to consider and use when navigating confrontational situations. To begin, the first section examines questions to ask yourself as you enter the confrontation level.

QUESTIONS TO ASK YOURSELF

A move toward confrontation is a serious decision. By doing so, you are acknowledging that previous levels chosen to address and resolve the situation have not met with satisfactory results. Consequently, your initial concern remains, and it is likely that if not resolved, matters will worsen. In addition, because you consider the concern of major importance, you feel an urgency to address and resolve it so that, hopefully, a respectful relationship will survive and possibly thrive. However, we recognize that this is not always possible.

There are times when potentially harmful and hostile confrontations may occur. For example, when you confront a stranger on school property and that person is clearly under the influence of alcohol or drugs, the encounter could escalate. At times like these, you should summon help and protect students until the person is removed from campus. All of this requires teamwork and safety precautions, which we will address in Chapter 6.

Key Point 5.1

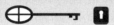

Moving from consultation to confrontation is not a step you should take lightly. Confrontation is a method that you only use when sincere attempts at less-risky levels have not succeeded.

This section offers five questions to consider when you are wondering whether to *confront* about an unresolved concern.

1. Have all lower levels been sincerely and honestly applied?

2. Does evidence exist that lower levels have not worked?

3. Who has the authority to follow through with consequences?

4. Does the will exist to confront?

5. Will confrontation elicit dependency?

These questions are not all inclusive of the information and answers desired to make a decision, but they provide a basis upon which you can begin contemplating the pros and cons of using confrontation in a relationship.

Question 1: Have all lower levels been sincerely and honestly applied?

This book has presented three preliminary levels in seeking desirable ends (concern, confer, and consult). The sincerity and trustfulness with which you apply each of the three lower levels—assessing a concern, conferring with people involved, and establishing a consulting relationship—are vital. Therefore, asking yourself how heartfelt and genuine your first attempts were is appropriate.

Conflicts tend to tax human emotions. One by-product of such stress on your emotions might include a lower commitment to the respect for yourself and others. You run roughshod over both. You think less of the person and take detrimental shortcuts. A second might be that you pay less attention to the integrity of the relationship. These two by-products counter the fundamental intention of resolving conflicts constructively with mutually beneficial outcomes.

True, not all conflicts are resolved in ways such that all parties view the outcomes as personally beneficial. As one employer said to a worker about to be fired, "I don't know how we will get along without you, but starting on Monday, we're going to find out." Still, one foundational belief of the Six-C Process is that the goal of mutual benefit is worth pursuing throughout the process. It demonstrates the value and integrity of each participant.

Asking the question of how honestly and sincerely you have expressed and processed a concern is a deeply personal one. Because you are asking it of yourself, you are in the best position to answer it truthfully. Supplemental to such an answer could be evidence that demonstrates you have sincerely acted on the three lower levels and they were insufficient to resolve the original concern. This leads to question two.

Question 2: Does evidence exist that lower levels have not worked?

When working through the Six-C Process, records that verify the previous levels you applied to address the concern, commitments made by you and others, strategies and interventions agreed upon to settle the situation, and progress made toward resolution and conciliation may be helpful in moving to higher levels of action. In some professional settings, this is required.

Evidence that you gather regarding these facts and events serves several purposes. First, it demonstrates the effort allotted to the process by you and others involved in the relationship. Second, it illustrates to some degree why particular steps and strategies did or did not succeed. In cases where evidence shows that lower-level efforts you attempted did not produce fruitful results in resolving the concern, you are more likely to be confident in moving to confront.

Evidences collected and compiled to demonstrate progress and commitment in all helping relationships is part of a professional and ethical stance to provide competent services. For some professionals, such as medical personnel, counselors, and therapists, records are regulated by the ethical codes of their respective professions, state statutes, and federal law (Gladding, 2009). In all cases of formal and informal recordkeeping, the ultimate purpose is to demonstrate sincere, honest, and competent practice for the welfare of all concerned.

Evidence might include asking relatives, friends, colleagues, and other professionals you trust to review the situation and serve as witnesses. This action may reveal that they, or someone they know, have encountered the same concern. Examination of such evidence helps you and other people involved determine what steps have been successful or not and whether confrontation is necessary.

If your decision leads to confrontation, an important assessment is to determine if you have the authority to implement consequences that would logically follow an unresolved concern. If you do not have such authority, find out who does. This introduces the third question.

Question 3: Who has the authority to follow through with consequences?

In families, schools, businesses, agencies, and other institutions of society, decisions made about applying consequences to specific actions are rendered by those empowered with appropriate authority. Burgess and Burgess (1997) noted that successful use of confrontation assumes that the role of power (authority) is unavoidable.

Key Point 5.2

Knowing what authority you have—its limits and extent—is imperative in selecting appropriate consequences to apply in the confrontation level.

Logical consequences, without the power and will to enforce them, are meaningless. At times, you may not have the authority to implement a desired consequence to address your concern. As one example, a classroom teacher who has been unsuccessful in ameliorating a concern about a student's frequent disruptive behavior does not have authority to remove the student from school. That authority rests with the school administration or school board.

Knowing what authority you have—its limits and extent—is imperative in selecting appropriate consequences to apply in the confrontation level of the Six-C Process. Attempting to resolve a concern by applying consequences, penalties, or other remedies that are not within your purview to administer jeopardizes the trust and integrity of a democratic helping relationship.

If you have the necessary authority to administer consequences related to an unresolved concern, then it is possible to confront with confidence. On the other hand, if you do not have the required authority, you will need to include other people who have it. For example, in the case of a teacher and disruptive student, the teacher might consult with the school principal about options and consequences available *before* confronting a disruptive student. Having the backing of the principal and the knowledge of what consequences might be applicable would give the teacher a stronger stance with which to move forward. Even when you have the authority to apply consequences, another ingredient to consider about confrontation is your desire to use it at all.

Question 4: Does the will exist to confront?

People accomplish little in life without the will to make things happen. This axiom is also true in your decision to confront another person about an unresolved concern. There are times when it is necessary to put people on notice that your concern is causing you serious and persistent personal or professional distress. Because confrontation includes psychological and emotional dynamics, you want to be certain of your desire to confront. Do you have the will to see the confrontation through to its conclusion and accept possible outcomes? There are risks involved. Some examples of risks when confronting include a backlash effect, escalation of the situation, and feelings of powerlessness (Burgess & Burgess, 1996, 1997). These are worth a closer look.

A backlash effect occurs when the consequences you apply through confrontation lead to resentment on the part of the person or persons that you confronted. Such resentment, when gone unchecked, can encourage resistant, or worse, vengeful behaviors that breed new concerns and ongoing conflict. In these instances, your initial concern might seem to be resolved, but damage caused by the resentment, resistance, and retaliation that follow far outweighs any positive gain you have made.

As an example of backlash, suppose you are a junior high school principal and have a concern regarding how teachers dress for school. After trying less-potent levels of resolving your concern—without success—you decide to confront the issue by asking the faculty to vote on a faculty dress code. You win the vote, a dress code for faculty is established, and you think the issue is settled; but a few teachers remain bitter and angry. You do not know what types of sabotage could be in store in the future. In this case, you might question if your decision to ask for a vote of the faculty is worth the potential backlash.

Escalation is another danger to consider when confronting someone about a concern. This consideration takes on special significance when confronting strangers. You never know what baggage they are carrying or what frustrations they are experiencing. Road rage is a common term to describe how some people explode with deadly anger over the slightest perceived offence or disrespect. It is always wise to approach strangers with caution. Sometimes, emotions override reason when confrontation incites and inflames, and consequently, relationships become contested battlegrounds rather than problem-solving venues. Instead of moving toward resolution and conciliation, they become arenas of hatred and violence. Avoiding such polarizing results is key to using confrontation for positive, mutual gain.

Question 5: Will confrontation elicit dependency?

All helping relationships include the inherent risk of becoming a vehicle for dependency. As you move toward confrontation, a more direct and forceful process with which to address a concern, the question of dependency versus responsibility is appropriate to consider. The use of authority and power sometimes elicits responses of submission and powerlessness; both of which can be requisites to unintended dependency on you (the person of authority) who expressed the initial concern. An example might be helpful here.

> *Suppose that a mother and her adolescent daughter have had ongoing discussions about the daughter's choice of friends, particularly boy friends. The mother has expressed her concern frequently, then moved to more formal consulting processes, and finally has decided to confront her daughter using preset consequences if the girl insists on violating family values and breaking rules. One of the risks the mother takes in using power-laden confrontation is that the daughter may become too submissive and dependent on the mother's approval of her choice of friends and friendship behaviors. On the opposite pole, the mother also risks an angry, belligerent, and deviant reaction from the daughter that could become dangerous to herself or the mother. Together, the mother and daughter participate in this delicate balancing act, letting each one be responsible for their role. Being conscious of the risks of dependency or defiance will help the mother maintain a balanced perspective, monitoring the situation while watching for signals that her daughter may be seeking too much approval or rebelling in dangerous ways. The ideal outcome is for the daughter to take charge of her own value system, make healthy decisions about friendships, and rely on her mother's counsel when necessary and appropriate.*

An illusion of powerlessness occurs when confronted people perceive themselves as holding less power or authority within the relationship than actually exists (Burgess & Burgess, 1996). In many school situations, for example, students seemingly hold less power and authority than administrators, teachers, and other professionals. The illusion of powerlessness is risky because it frequently leads to withdrawal, dependency, submission, lack of self-respect, or injustice, none of which contributes to a healthy, productive resolution of concerns.

One way for you to contend with people's feelings of powerlessness is to advocate on their behalf. In schools, for example, student advocacy is a role of professional counselors who often mediate concerns among students, between students and teachers, and even among faculty and staff (Schmidt, 2008). When feelings of powerlessness remain unchecked and untreated, questions of dependency may interfere with growth and development.

Key Point 5.3

When you choose to confront, you are making a serious attempt to either resolve or manage a troublesome concern. As such, confrontation is an appropriate practice to use within a broader scope of a conflict.

All five of the above questions give you a framework with which to decide whether it is appropriate to confront another person about a concern. Beyond appropriateness, these questions may also provide information and insight about the likelihood that by using confrontation, you will obtain the desired outcome. Before proceeding, it is worth your time to consider the differences between conflict and confrontation. Having an appreciation of the difference between conflict and confrontation is a first step in gaining greater understanding of what it means *to confront.*

DIFFERENCE BETWEEN CONFLICT AND CONFRONTATION

Conflict, described earlier in this book, includes a wide range of wants, strategies, interests, styles, and viewpoints. It encompasses disagreement about behavior, ideas, principles, and a host of other perspectives. In contrast, confrontation is the act of asserting yourself and your responsibilities when a significant concern remains unresolved.

Because the Six-C Process adheres to democratic principles, the tools and approaches you select to address a concern are required to meet criteria that fit with such principles. Then, you apply them with respect for the persons in the process.

It may be helpful to pause here and revisit the principle of economy that we introduced in Chapter 2. The principle is that you begin with the simplest explanation of an event and move to complex ones only as necessary to address a concern. For example, the simplest way to review the accuracy of a check given by a waiter in a restaurant is to use arithmetic. However, for increasingly complex problems, such as calculating a city's use of energy, you may need to move upward to algebra or higher mathematical processes.

Within larger conflicts that consist of many concerns, confrontation should seek to address only one concern at a time. Confront a person about one concern within a conflict, while holding other concerns in reserve for future consideration.

In addition to using the previous five questions to help structure a decision about whether to confront and knowing the differences between conflict and confrontation, you also want to have some understanding and command of clear communication skills. The next section offers a brief summary and analysis of some important skills to use in confrontations.

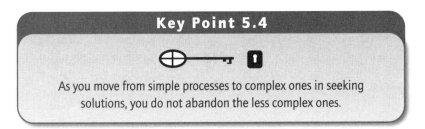

Key Point 5.4

As you move from simple processes to complex ones in seeking solutions, you do not abandon the less complex ones.

CONTINUING IMPORTANCE OF CLEAR COMMUNICATION

As noted, clear communication is necessary for successful application of the Six-C Process, and this is particularly so when using confrontation. An earlier chapter highlighted several valuable communication skills that are helpful in applying the Six-C Process. In addition to those highlighted earlier, skills to facilitate successful confrontation include monitoring emotions, resisting bias, managing time, controlling the pace, and avoiding arguments (Burgess & Burgess, 1996). A description about each will help to explain their meanings.

Monitoring Emotions

To use confrontation successfully, you seek to stay calm in the heat of battle. This is particularly important when dealing with anger but also has value in keeping other emotions in check, such as fear and sadness. It is nearly impossible to communicate clearly and respectfully when you allow unbridled emotions to propel your thoughts and actions.

There is an abundance of information on how to control your emotions. You can find suggestions on the Internet, in many books and articles, and in various sections of this book (see Chapters 2, 3, 4, and 6). A quick review of available research suggests you stay calm, listen to your physical signals, and allow the person to vent by using strategic silence (see "climbing the emotion mountain" in the next chapter). One specific suggestion on how to control your emotions not mentioned elsewhere is to redirect the discussion. Sometimes during a confrontation, it may be helpful to move to a related topic that does not have the same level of emotional energy. Moving from the primary concern to a less threatening one does not violate our axiom of "One concern at a time." Here we are temporarily shifting the primary concern to focus on another, less emotional one. You can do this after accepting the person's feelings and suggesting that you consider other related issues. A statement such as, "I can see how important this is to you and wonder if we might discuss a related problem that might help us resolve this one."

The preceding suggestions are not intended to be used all at once. Consider using each of them in concert with other communication skills to help control your emotions during stressful confrontations.

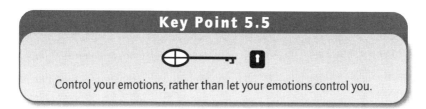

Key Point 5.5

Control your emotions, rather than let your emotions control you.

Resisting Bias

Keep all your communication at a respectful level. Avoid stereotypical remarks, negative body language, or prejudicial references to groups of people. Such behaviors are examples of bias that communicates disrespect. When you assume that stereotypes are accurate, you foster unfortunate outcomes. Consider the following illustration:

At the beginning of the new school year, a young teacher was warned about two students who would be in her class. She was told that one student would cry at the least excuse, while the other was a bully who terrorized fellow students. When school began and the students arrived, the teacher was able to spot the two difficult students. One wore heavy metal T-shirts and a leather coat, had a mohawk haircut, and weighed about 180 pounds. The other was an apparently meek little fellow who was quiet as a mouse. The teacher did a good job spotting the two students she was warned about, except that she had it backwards. The big fellow was the crybaby, while the little student was the holy terror.

A Chinese student of one of the authors reminded him of the importance of cultural sensitivity. When the author referred to Asians as "Orientals," the student quickly responded, "Dr. Purkey, oriental is a rug!" Avoiding bias requires continuous recalibration of thinking.

Managing Time

Your ability to stay aware of the time available is a valuable attribute in facilitating most human relationships. It takes on added importance when confronting someone about an ongoing concern. Time is finite, so structuring the time you have available within a confrontation is helpful in communicating clearly your expectations and the consequences involved.

Key Point 5.6

Managing time is a valuable attribute in facilitating most human relationships, and it takes on added importance when confronting someone about an ongoing concern.

A good way to manage time is to set limits. For example, suppose a parent shows up at your school unannounced and wants to talk with you. You explain that you have 10 minutes before you must be in class, and that 10 minutes is devoted to the parent. At the end of the 10 minutes, you assertively excuse yourself and go to class.

Controlling the Pace

Related to time management is your awareness of the tempo of a relationship. Because confrontation can involve many powerful emotions, sometimes there is a tendency to accelerate the pace. The opposite, slowing down the pace, may be more helpful because it gives both parties of the confrontation time to consider all that has been stated and presented.

Avoiding Arguments

An additional way to control the pace of confrontation is by avoiding unnecessary, distracting arguments. As we noted in Chapter 1, encouraging arguments is seldom productive. By avoiding them, you maintain control of the pace and direction of the confrontation at hand.

Each of the above behaviors can enhance clear communication. More importantly, in concert with other skills, they help to present confrontation as a beneficial process—a positive force. Confronting may damage a relationship, but it can also strengthen it.

CONFRONTATION AS A POSITIVE FORCE

Literature about direct and assertive behaviors in education and leadership in recent years has focused on its positive use (Burgess & Burgess, 1996, 1997; Hoover & DiSilvestro, 2005; O'Flynn & Kennedy, 2000). A common phrase to describe this movement is *constructive confrontation.* Simply stated, constructive confrontation is a notion of using confrontation while controlling and minimizing destructive elements. At the same time, constructive confrontation aims at maximizing beneficial outcomes—building up rather than tearing down. The next section of this chapter offers a brief summary of constructive confrontation and ways to adapt it when applying the Six-C Process.

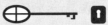
ADAPTING CONSTRUCTIVE CONFRONTATION

The idea of constructive confrontation emerged from work and study in the Conflict Research Consortium at the University of Colorado (Burgess & Burgess, 1996). Other theorists and practitioners have adapted the concept (Hoover & DiSilvestro, 2005; O'Flynn & Kennedy, 2000). Because the assumptions infused with constructive confrontation align with those of the Six-C Process, we have adapted some of these for this book. A first assumption is that confrontation is a platform that offers opportunity for growth and development for all parties.

Opportunity for Growth

A myth of confrontation is that it brings about only negative results. From the perspective of the Six-C Process, to confront means to face something or someone intentionally with beneficial purpose. Constructive confrontation has the potential to establish relationships through which people can learn problem-solving behaviors and communication skills and apply them to other circumstances and situations throughout life. Equally important, there are psychological advantages in finding courage to confront others regarding your legitimate concern.

Imagine a colleague who continuously interrupts when you are speaking. This has become a concern to you. You have tried conferring and consulting with little effect, so you decide to firmly assert yourself. The next time your colleague interrupts, you stop and state firmly, "I appreciate your point of view. It is important that you let me finish my thought." This assertive behavior is likely to strengthen your self-respect and give your colleague pause to reflect on his or her behavior.

Even when the consequences applied through constructive confrontation are unpleasant in the eyes of one or more participants, there remains opportunity for learning and development. When you use confrontation with utmost regard for all parties, attention to issues of safety and welfare and appreciation for the abilities and value of all involved, people will more likely accept this opportunity for reflection and growth.

An aspect of constructive confrontation that keeps the door open for opportunities to learn and develop is the focus on reframing the problem (Burgess & Burgess, 1997). Chapter 4 of this book mentioned the value of reframing (reconceptualization) in addressing concerns, so the following section gives a brief review of how reframing can enhance the use of confrontation.

Another Look at Reframing

Frequently, conflicts escalate and become seemingly unsolvable because of the way we frame a concern, problem, or situation. Burgess and Burgess (1996) referred to "muddled framing" to describe how people become confused about what the concern is and their position regarding it. Another aspect of framing a concern involves the divergent perceptions each person has about the situation. As emphasized in Chapter 1, perceptions are key elements in helping people draw conclusions about themselves, others, and life events. Therefore, by stating and framing concerns clearly and with understanding by all parties, you create a key ingredient for successful confrontation.

In reframing a concern, you might find two strategic ideas helpful. The first is to break the concern down into smaller issues and goals rather than focusing on a larger and possibly unreasonable objective. For example, if the concern of a parent is to help a child achieve academic success in school, a smaller, incremental goal, such as monitoring time spent playing on the computer or watching TV, could assist in framing the goal of improving the child's performance. Try the exercises that follow.

You are meeting with a parent who has not followed through on a promise to ensure that their child completes daily homework assignments. The parent has numerous excuses. Use this exercise to reframe both the teacher's goals and the parent's excuses. At times, reframing can be useful from either perspective.

(Continued)

(Continued)

The teacher says, "Your child is not going to get promoted unless you can ensure that she completes every homework assignment for the rest of the year."

Your reframing: _____

The teacher says, "Can you set a time every evening to spend with your child and ensure that homework is completed?"

Your reframing: _____

The parent says, "I have five children and hold down two jobs. It's impossible to keep track of her homework too."

Your reframing: _____

The parent says, "I don't understand why homework is important if you teach her for six hours a day!"

Your reframing: _____

The second strategy for reframing is to keep an eye on long-term benefits of resolving the concern rather than focusing on minor arguments and skirmishes. For example, during a parent–teacher conference, a counselor might explain to the parents that the school and parents are partners in helping the child. This might reframe the conversation. In other words, frame the big picture rather than dispute the details of color and composition. Try the following exercise and reframe what is said to capture the bigger picture.

A student says, "This math is so hard. I just don't see why algebra is important to me becoming a lawyer."

Your reframing: _____

A parent says, "My child's teacher seems to spend too much time helping students who are slow learners."

Your reframing: _____

In using both of these strategies, breaking down larger concerns into smaller goals and keeping an eye on the big picture, you will also find it useful to stick to basic facts so that reframing provides an accurate portrayal of the situation.

Stick to the Facts

Handling conflicts and resorting to confrontation frequently incite emotions. When this happens, we sometimes sacrifice logic and fact. Constructive confrontation depends on the use of factual statements (O'Flynn & Kennedy, 2000). By sticking to the facts and logically expressing the concern, you are more likely to keep emotions in check. Consequently, the person or persons hearing your concern are better able to receive it calmly. Consider these two responses by a teacher to the same situation. A student yells out, "Math is stupid!"

First response: "Billy, you must stop disrupting the class with your silly outbursts!"

Second response: "Billy, you said that 'Math is stupid.'"

The first response addresses the concern with value judgments—*disrupting class* and *silly outbursts.* The second more precisely states the fact of what the student said. Because the first response invites escalation of conflict, the teacher faces a greater challenge in framing a concern. In contrast, the second response simply states what happened and sets a stronger foundation upon which to frame the student's comment (your concern) and proceed to logical consequences for the student's behavior.

Sticking to the facts of a situation allows everyone involved to monitor their feelings and remain relatively calm. This is helpful because it avoids escalation of a conflict that could better be handled at lower levels of the Six-C Process. By keeping feelings at even keel, you also prevent procedural problems from overshadowing your primary concern.

Procedural Problems

When conflicts escalate, people tend to pay less attention to expected procedures. Often, in the heat of battle people ignore rules; and subsequently, participants feel betrayed and treated unfairly. Such feelings lower their expectation for success and threaten the likelihood that they will cooperate. The Six-C Process uses constructive confrontation while placing a high premium on procedures. Through every step of a confrontation, you ensure that all parties are aware of procedures, regulations, and processes that may have a bearing on the outcome. In schools, this is particularly important because of local policies, state regulations, and federal laws that could have a connection with the concern.

Realistic Outcomes

Although constructive confrontation begins with a positive perspective, it maintains a realistic view of potential outcomes. It is constructive in its approach and avoids destructive behaviors; but at the same time, we understand that when the conflict is resolved, some participants might feel less than euphoric about the process and the outcome. While a goal of constructive confrontation is to provide a growth experience for all involved, sometimes such growth comes through difficult lessons with much sweat and tears. Not all parties in all situations will feel like winners. This is because the person for whom you intend the consequences typically has little control over the application of these penalties; you do.

Logical Consequences

Rudolf Dreikurs (1968; Dreikurs & Grey, 1968) was one of the first authorities to write about logical consequences. A disciple of Alfred Adler (1954), Dreikurs explained that both natural consequences and logical consequences follow ill-advised behaviors.

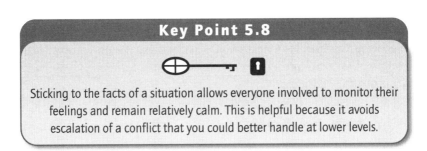

Key Point 5.8

Sticking to the facts of a situation allows everyone involved to monitor their feelings and remain relatively calm. This is helpful because it avoids escalation of a conflict that you could better handle at lower levels.

Natural consequences are negative outcomes of behavior that require no intervention from another person. For example, if a child jumps on a bed, he or she might end up with a bumped head or broken bed. Similarly, if a parent carelessly uses the stove, he or she might get burned or cause a fire.

Logical consequences of behavior are outcomes connected to the behavior through "the purposeful intervention of another person" (Sweeney, 1998, p. 114). In democratic societies, natural consequences are complemented by logical consequences, which are the results of rules and laws being applied to behavioral offenses. For instance, if you drive your car like a maniac, you may get a ticket (logical consequence), or worse, you may injure or kill yourself and innocent bystanders (natural consequences).

Constructive confrontation relies on the reasonable and fair application of logical consequences. Natural consequences and logical consequences work in tandem to establish useful outcomes to behavior through which people can learn and make beneficial choices for future development. The following example illustrates natural and logical consequences regarding the same concern.

> *An adolescent comes home too late for dinner, which begins at 6:00 p.m. by family agreement. The family has agreed that if a member is late for a meal, he or she misses that course and waits until the next meal. For the adolescent in this family, being late for dinner means that the next meal is breakfast, which is the logical consequence. The natural consequence of being late is that the adolescent will be hungry until morning.*

Logical consequences have an important place in constructive confrontation. They are the agreed-upon rules or existing regulations (e.g., board of education policy and state law), which are enforced to resolve a concern. Consistent and fair application of logical consequences is paramount to their success. By contrast, inconsistent and unfair application of consequences is illogical and undemocratic—two unacceptable conditions for the Six-C Process.

Enabling Undermines Responsibility

As used here, *enabling* is the act of doing something or not doing something that allows someone to continue an irresponsible pattern of behavior or to avoid a responsibility he or she has. People often begin enabling actions in an attempt to be kind and helpful. For example, a parent might constantly wake an adolescent student so he or she does not miss the school bus. In this case, the parent is assuming the adolescent's responsibility to get up and catch the bus and subsequently is enabling the child to be irresponsible.

One problem when you fail to confront is the danger of enabling someone inappropriately and undermining responsibility. Enabling takes place when you give extensions to timelines, encourage others to expect productive outcomes with no work or little effort, do things for others that they are able to do for themselves, or fail to hold others accountable for their decisions and behaviors. In contrast, when you confront others about timelines, work habits, effort, and their accountability, you provide an excellent opportunity for their development and growth.

There is a learning process in teaching responsibility. For example, when you

- Go outdoors, it saves heating or cooling energy if you shut the door;
- Borrow someone's tools, it shows respect to return them promptly;
- Leave a room, it saves money to turn the lights out;
- Are finished riding your bicycle, it is safest to put it away;
- Drop something on the floor, prevent accidents by picking it up;
- Use the copy machine, help others by refilling the paper tray;
- Watch TV, keep the sound at a respectful level;
- Make a mess, clean it up so others may use the space; and
- Have appointments, be on time out of respect for everyone else.

Young people tend to respond to parents, teachers, and other adults who model high standards and expect the same, coupled with personal interest and respect. The following illustration of enabling took place in a middle school.

At lunchtime, students left so much trash on the tables and the floor that the principal had to hire a part-time sweeper to clean up after them. The students accepted no responsibility for keeping the cafeteria clean. A new principal took over the school and announced that the PTA donated money for the school to use. She informed the students that they could take responsibility for keeping the cafeteria free of trash after their lunchtime, and if they did, the money saved from not having to hire extra custodial care could be used for an end-of-the-year field trip to a favorite location. Students accepted the responsibility and incentive. From that point until the end of the year, the cafeteria, after lunch, was free of trash.

The previous sections of this chapter provided a brief summary of confrontation with a particular perspective on applying constructive confrontation within the Six-C Process. As noted, confrontations of any type can illicit strong emotions. Therefore, *to confront* in a constructive manner you want to be responsible and at the same time be positive and compassionate. The next section offers a few practical ideas for confronting in a constructive manner.

APPLYING FIVE PRACTICAL TIPS

In handling conflicts, no strategy is fail-safe. You can never be 100% certain of what will happen in a confrontation. By being prepared, taking time to understand the situation, increasing your awareness of the physical side of emotions, using attentive communication skills, and appreciating the full impact of a confrontation, you can increase the likelihood of resolving a concern. This is particularly true when confronting a concern head on. The following five tips point out ways to place yourself in a stronger and more positive position when confronting others about a concern.

1. Be aware of body language
2. Rehearse your concern
3. Stay focused
4. Listen carefully
5. Be empathic

1. Be Aware of Body Language

Many physical symptoms correlate with the emotions associated with confrontation. Increased heartbeat, perspiration, and adrenaline are a few reactions. For example, when working with a student who has clenched teeth, is frowning, has hunched-back shoulders, crossed arms and legs, and tells you he is fine, believe the actions you observe and not necessarily the words you hear. As another illustration of being aware of body language, police officers train to stand obliquely to a suspect rather than facing directly, which in Western culture is a typical prelude to physical combat.

By taking time to understand how you respond to confrontation, you are in a stronger position to control yourself. Before assuming a confrontation posture, for example, you might do breathing exercises or meditation to calm down and develop a sense of body control. Rehearsing by thinking about what you plan to say in the upcoming confrontation is also helpful.

2. Rehearse Your Concern

Practice may not make perfect when confronting another person, but rehearsing what to say makes good sense. When we confront without forethought, we tend to say things in haste and often find that matters are worse or we have spawned regrettable results. A wise colleague once remarked that if you tend to say the first thing that pops into your head, you will give the greatest speech you will forever regret. Taking time to rehearse what to say, and even watching oneself in a mirror while saying it, can be productive practice. Few people act well without a script, so practicing your lines may make a better performance! Practicing will also help you to remain calm in confrontational situations. In their book, *Managing Conversations With Hostile Parents,* Kosmoski and Pollack (2001) gave valuable tips on maintaining personal control. An adaptation of these suggestions includes

- Controlling both your voice and choice of words;
- Understanding that the hostility you hear is not about you personally;
- Sticking to the facts (the particulars) of the event;
- Using breathing and distancing techniques; and
- Planning a collection of appropriate comebacks to use.

Key Point 5.9

Practice may not make perfect when confronting another person, but rehearsing what to say makes good sense.

3. Stay Focused

Successful confrontation takes considerable skill, energy, and attention. Distractions can get in the way by interfering with the focus of the moment. By remaining alert, keeping the mind uncluttered, watching closely, and staying on task and subject, you are in stronger position to behave intentionally and in the best interest of all involved.

4. Listen Carefully

As noted throughout this book, communication skills are essential in using all of the Six Cs. Among the most important communication skills is *listening,* and its value is of particular importance when confronting another person. Speaking directly and honestly sets a trustworthy tone in a confrontation. Equally important, however, is your ability and willingness to listen. In a confrontation, it is probably a good rule to speak slowly and briefly while listening fully and empathically.

5. Be Empathic

Seeking to understand the feelings and perceptions of other people is a vital attribute in using constructive confrontation. Empathic relationships are not ones that focus on right or wrong but rather on the concerns and beliefs of all involved. To confront another person with a high level of empathic understanding will likely decrease the intensity of the confrontation. Although we cannot entirely eliminate combat, we can influence its nature and impact.

SUMMARY

This chapter presented the fourth level of the Six-C Process, *confront.* This level addressed the most difficult types of concerns that resist lower levels of resolution and remain unresolved. It explored questions to consider before deciding to use confrontation and examined aspects of confrontation to gain a greater understanding of this high-stakes level. An approach called *constructive confrontation* was introduced and presented as a means of offering practical ideas for confronting in a positive manner.

In rare instances, the levels described thus far in this book may not produce the desired results. When this is the case, you may decide to play a very high card indeed: *combat.* This high level of concern is the topic of our next chapter.

Key Point 5.10

Understanding the feelings and perceptions of other people is a vital attribute in using constructive confrontation. Empathic relationships are not ones that focus on right or wrong but rather on the concerns and beliefs of all involved.

Major Themes

- *Confrontation* is a serious level of action that you should not take lightly or use without careful consideration. Several questions offered in this chapter may help you decide whether this course of action is appropriate and necessary to address your concern.
- People sometimes confuse *conflict* with *confrontation.* Here, we differentiate the two by presenting confrontation as a process (a level) for dealing with conflict.
- *Constructive confrontation* is a particular view of using confrontation in ways that improves relationships, provides opportunities for growth, uses logical consequences, seeks realistic outcomes, and calls upon other positive behaviors to address concerns at this level of action.
- By rehearsing and practicing various constructive behaviors, you place yourself in a stronger position to use confrontation successfully when the occasion calls for it.

CHAPTER SIX

Combat

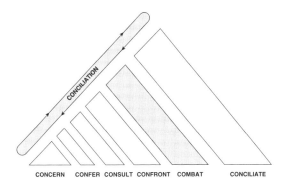

CONCERN CONFER CONSULT CONFRONT COMBAT   CONCILIATE

Suppose you are a young principal of an inner-city middle school. One of your veteran teachers is causing concern by abusive, insulting, and seemingly racist teaching practices. Students often leave class in tears, and their parents, guardians, and other adult caregivers are up in arms. You have conferred, consulted, and confronted this teacher. Nothing has changed. The teacher is convinced that this approach is the "only language these kids understand." Is it time for combat?

In this chapter, we define *combat* as significant friction between and among people based on divergent perceptions and/or opposing desires. We also interpret combat as a major effort to reduce or eliminate a concern by following through with specific consequential actions. Used in this way, combat becomes a verb, not a noun. The goal is to combat a troublesome situation, not go to war with people.

CONSTRAINTS ON COMBAT

As stated in earlier chapters, combat is a very high and often dangerous card to play. The use of the word *combat* stresses the seriousness of the situation. It suggests that all earlier attempts to resolve a significant concern have failed. Because we are at the point in our concern where confer, consult, and confront have not produced desired results, it is now time to move to a very strong C—combat.

Unfortunately, trying to manage a troublesome situation through combat can easily become a win/lose situation. Who wins and who loses is never a sure bet.

> There is a story of King Xerxes in Ancient Persia who decided to invade Greece. To ensure that this was a wise move, the King traveled to Delphi and consulted the Oracles, who were famous throughout the ancient world for predicting the future. When the King asked if he should invade, the Oracles replied, "Oh, King, if you invade Greece a mighty empire will fall." Taking this as an assurance of victory, the King invaded Greece. The Greeks soundly defeated his armies and King Xerxes' mighty empire fell. The Oracles were right.

When considering whether to combat a situation, placing constraints and limitations on your decision are necessary for many reasons. Combat demands a great deal of time, energy, and resources. Once again, ask yourself, "Am I convinced that my concern is of sufficient importance to move to the level of combat? If the answer is yes, then perhaps a move to this high level is unavoidable.

The combat level raises many philosophical and practical issues for you to consider. After all, combat is usually associated with fights and struggles among people. Such designations seem contrary to the civility and respectfulness that we emphasize in the Six-C Process. When applied respectfully, however, it is congruent with the basic humane tenets of this process.

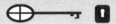

Key Point 6.1

When considering whether to combat a situation, placing constraints and limitations on your decision are necessary for many reasons. Combat demands a great deal of time, energy, and resources.

PUNISHMENTS, PENALTIES, AND PERCEPTIONS

It is our belief that the combat level of the Six-C Process can exist without hostility, punitive action, or harsh penalties. In Chapter 5, we explained how the use of logical consequences assists us when applying constructive confrontation to resolve or remedy a concern. This concept holds true for combat as well. Behaviors that belittle, demean, hurt, or otherwise rob people of their dignity are unnecessary conditions to use at the combat level within the context of the Six-C Process. This is not to say that you can be permissive, uncertain, lax, acquiescent, or without authority when implementing strategies at this level of concern. Reaching a desirable outcome at this level depends on your assured assertiveness. As Nel Noddings (1995), a noted advocate for caring in education, commented, "There are times when you just gotta do it." Strength is an essential quality in maintaining a respectful and trustworthy posture.

Although diminished and judicious use of punishments and penalties is central to the Six-C Process, the perceptions of those involved heavily influences how these actions are viewed. Thus, your most respectful, fair administration of logical consequences may be perceived by others as harsh, disrespectful, and unjust. For example, imagine the reaction of fans when a football team is penalized for the behavior of an unruly coach. They boo the official—not the coach.

Understanding this relationship between consequences and perceptions helps you remain grounded in the reality of a combat situation. Even the most logical, even-handed, and respectful consequences may be received and acted upon grudgingly. Expecting people to accept responsibility, live up to their commitments, and follow through on obligations does not necessarily extinguish the plea, "You're not being fair!" Nevertheless, your consistent and dependable application of consequences is likely to win favor over the long haul, and you often will receive judgment of fairness among those with whom you attempt to build working relationships.

Your use of logical consequences and other outcomes related to ill-advised behaviors will be more effective if you keep an open posture about how the other person perceives these actions. All of this relates to the way you apply what authority you have in the combat relationship.

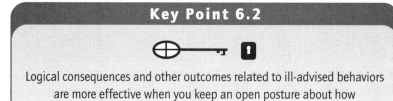

Key Point 6.2

Logical consequences and other outcomes related to ill-advised behaviors are more effective when you keep an open posture about how the other person perceives these actions.

Perceptions of unfair treatment can elicit the strongest feelings of anger, fear, or sadness. Frequently, people manifest these feelings with defiance and hostility. When faced with such behaviors, it is reasonable for you to consider the possibility that the other person may have, in fact, been treated unfairly. If upon reflection you decide that the anger, fear, or sadness is justified, then you will want to seek ways to make amends. This may include an expression of regret and, when appropriate, an apology. This is followed by efforts to make amends.

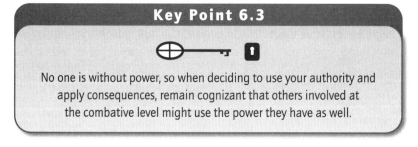

Key Point 6.3

No one is without power, so when deciding to use your authority and apply consequences, remain cognizant that others involved at the combative level might use the power they have as well.

INCREASING CHANCES
FOR A DESIRABLE OUTCOME

When professionals such as educators are called upon to face conflict, they might be wise to turn to an unusual source for advice: the United States Naval War College. The College teaches officers how to evaluate and cope with the most challenging situations. The Navy's formula is O2S4MEC. The formula is quite complex, but it has been simplified by one of the authors into the acronym SUNSET (Purkey, 1996). The six-point acronym provides a mnemonic technique for assisting your memory:

- Superiority at point of contact
- Unity of command
- Navigational mobility
- Simplicity of plan
- Economy of force
- Targeted objective

With modifications, SUNSET is useful in describing how to handle conflicts at the combat level in the most reasonable and productive manner. Let us look at the six points of SUNSET more closely.

Key Point 6.4

As you combat a situation, it will be in your best interest to assume only the authority that comes with your personal integrity or professional position, and apply the power associated with your authority respectfully, ethically, and with great care.

Superiority at Point of Contact

The primary source of a satisfactory resolution of a conflict is superior documentation. In every way possible, you want to be able to demonstrate that you have used each of the four lower C's of the Six-C Process (concern, confer, consult, and confront) in attempting to address the original concern. Document that you have carefully reviewed your concern to ensure that it is significant, that you have moved patiently from concern to confer, to consult, to confront, and that now you are, reluctantly, at the combat level. Reluctance is a key component here because you want to avoid the appearance of having sprung hastily into a combative position.

Where possible, be able to document your efforts with witnesses. Support your concern from numerous sources. Record dates, times, and places where you made earlier efforts but failed to achieve the desired outcome. In personal concerns, enlist family and friends to verify your earlier efforts to ameliorate your concern. With professional concerns, you might rely on supervisors, colleagues, ombudsmen, and in the most serious of situations, an attorney.

In your school or agency, find out what policies exist regarding the keeping of anecdotal records. These records are of great help when a establishing a timeline of what has already taken place.

In the United States, most schools and agencies have policies regarding recordkeeping, and there are local, state, and federal laws, such as the Family Education Rights and Privacy Act of 1974, that you will want to follow. If you are a professional in a school or agency, obtain a copy of school or agency policies and procedures regarding the concern. Sometimes, lack of awareness of important policies and procedures can unravel plans and strategies that would otherwise be productive.

Keep in mind that people are likely to become angry when they believe that others are trying to control them, particularly in combat situations. For this reason, keep a careful record and be quick to ask for help when needed. It may be difficult to combat a situation by yourself. Seek support and assistance when appropriate and use the perceptions of others as a sounding board before moving forward.

Superiority at point of contact can also mean to match or outnumber your potential opponents during a meeting. For example, if a delegation of four individuals insists on having a group meeting with you, you would be wise to ask four or five of your colleagues to join the meeting. This might include the school counselor, psychologist, social worker, teachers, and administrators. Knowing you have your own team on the field can be a comfort in combat situations.

One additional point to consider about superiority at point of contact is to be aware of the potential for a violent encounter.

Angry people can lose control, and they come in all sizes and shapes. As Kosmoski and Pollack (2001) pointed out, age, sex, and physical appearance are not in and of themselves indicators of individuals who can be a genuine danger and threat to the safety of you and others in the school or agency.

Assess your strengths and abilities to deal effectively with extremely difficult situations. Identify your backups, security, police, and other resources, and be ready to contact them quickly if needed. Here are some basic rules to follow when faced with a very angry person and potentially explosive situation:

- Calm other individuals by your behavior
- Avoid touching an angry person
- Slow the pace of interaction and verbal delivery to avoid escalation
- Redirect to points of agreement
- Let the person "climb the emotion mountain"

Nothing is lost by allowing the person to express his or her feelings. Conversely, if you interfere with the full expression of feelings, the person will experience even greater anger, fear, or sadness. As explained by Podemski and Childers (1991) in their book on how to deal with angry people, it is important to give people the opportunity to express their anger completely. The full expression of feelings provides a catharsis for the person involved and may reduce negative feelings. Moreover, allowing the person to climb the emotion mountain might ease the tenseness of a combative situation. *Climbing the emotion mountain* requires a more detailed explanation.

As suggested, when a person is extremely angry, you are wise to let him or her vent fully without interruption. This means that you offer *no* apologies, *no* explanations, *no* arguments, *no* lectures, *no* placating, *no* agreement, and *no* defense. You listen carefully as the person climbs the emotion mountain. When the person arrives at the top, he or she will usually pause, take a breath, and begin to travel down the other side of the mountain to a less-heated stance.

Imagine that you are a high school principal and you are visited by a very angry parent. It seems her teenage daughter was kicked off the school bus for unruly behavior. The student had to walk home in the rain. The parent is furious. What should you do? After the parent has vented, paraphrase as much as you can remember of what the parent said. (Remember from Chapter 3 that paraphrasing is giving back to the person what you heard, in different words and form.) Paraphrasing shows that

1. You have been listening carefully (it is impossible to paraphrase without listening carefully);

2. You have heard the parent accurately (if you paraphrase inaccurately, the person will tell you);

3. The two of you are talking about the same thing; and

4. You have clear focus on the situation.

Unified Command

As a final reminder, the original troublesome situation is *your* concern. In other words, it is *your* dog. Here is an episode to illustrate the concept of ownership.

> *One of the authors greatly enjoys long walks with his wife. When they take a walk, a neighbor's dog sometimes follows them through the park. There is a leash law in the city where they live. When they pass another person with his or her dog on a leash, the author and his wife are given silent but deadly frowns. Nonverbally, the other person asks, "Why don't you have your damn dog on a leash? The looks and frowns became so painful that the author and his wife would explain emphatically, "It is not our dog!" Naturally, their neighbor's dog did nothing to dissuade the skeptical reactions. He seemed to enjoy the charade!*

Key Point 6.5

When a person is extremely angry, you are wise to
let him or her vent fully, without interruption.

In the case of your concern, it *is* your dog. There should be no question that it is *your* concern and therefore *your* responsibility. Once you have decided that your concern is sufficiently important to warrant combat, it is your responsibility to take command.

An example of unified command is the decision of many school administrators to assign an official spokesperson. This individual is the only one authorized to speak on behalf of the entire school system. In time of conflict or crisis, the official representative has the responsibility to present valid information to the public. This greatly reduces the spread of rumors, which tend to run wild during stressful situations.

Navigational Mobility

Maintaining flexibility for different situations requires different strategies. Make sure there is sufficient room to maneuver. Keep in mind an avenue of retreat, if necessary—as the adage suggests, "Never enter a room without exits." Give special attention to what-if questions. Here are a few examples in school settings to illustrate how you might consider what if.

- What if parents challenge the school discipline policies in court?
- What if students revolt and refuse to abide by a new dress code?
- What if a student comes to school with a gun?
- What if an angry parent insults you?
- What if the principal or superintendent does not back you up?
- What if a colleague accuses you of sexual harassment?
- What if you eject a student from class with the public declaration, "You are never coming back to this classroom!"— and the next day the principal returns the student to your room?
- What if someone threatens physical violence?

In planning a combat situation, it is important to consider as many outcomes as possible. Not just what *might* happen, but what *could* happen. What realistic options are available? Have you thought about, rehearsed, and implemented alternative plans if needed. There is a military axiom that battles are a succession of errors and mistakes on both sides. The victory goes to the side that makes the fewest blunders. Sooner or later, the worst set of conditions is bound to occur, so be prepared.

Navigational mobility also means to avoid making threats that you cannot carry out. Countless people have delivered ultimatums that have backfired. To illustrate, a talented high school student demands a larger role in a school play or he will quit the cast. The drama teacher calls his bluff and the student finds himself without any part in the play.

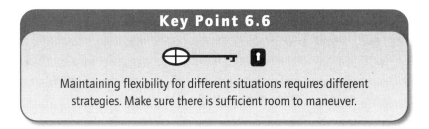

Key Point 6.6

Maintaining flexibility for different situations requires different strategies. Make sure there is sufficient room to maneuver.

Simplicity of Plan

The fewer moving parts in any machine, the less likely one part will fail. Likewise, in addressing a concern, you want to keep things as simple, straightforward, and as positive as possible. For example, if your concern deals with requiring students to keep their hands to themselves, be specific and direct in what you want in positive terms. Rather than place the situation in negative terms ("Don't touch or hit fellow students"), you would state, "Please keep your hands to yourself." Clearly stated and well-rehearsed directives ensure clear communication.

The value of simplicity of plan was experienced some years ago when one of the authors was involved with placing student teachers in schools for a single day.

Over the years, a tremendous university bureaucracy had developed to handle this single day's placement. Before their visits, students were required to obtain a special form from the university. Each student gave this form to the host teacher who then used the form to verify a student's attendance. Next, the teacher gave the completed form back to the student.

The student then returned the form to the university. There, a secretary recorded the attendance data. These data eventually worked their way back to each respective student's database. The student's supervisor then entered the data into his or her supervisory records. The author suggested that it would be much less complicated to simply ask the student to verify his or her visit. The author's idea was accepted, the students appreciated the trust, and an entire university bureaucracy collapsed.

Economy of Power

Use sufficient power to get the job done, but no more. Don't bite when a simple growl will do. Avoid wasting power or using overkill. Conduct a realistic appraisal of what you need to resolve the conflict. Why use a battering ram to open a door, when a key works quite nicely? Using heavy penalties or harsh punishments for relatively minor offenses violates the principle of economy of force. Research on punishment and human behavior has consistently shown that harsh punishment usually results in only brief decreases in the undesired behavior. Eventually, the undesired behavior or a worse behavior returns (Primary Prevention Committee of the Healthcare Coalition on Violence, 2003). For this reason, you want to search for consequences that show promise of longer-lasting results. Equally important, it is effective to use consequences that teach new behaviors to replace old, undesirable ones.

Absolute and mindless policies also violate the principle of economy. For example, suppose a school has a zero-tolerance policy for guns in the school. Anyone caught with a gun is permanently expelled. Now suppose a student risks her life to take a gun from a distraught fellow student. The heroic student is on her way to the office to turn it in when she is apprehended carrying the gun and is promptly expelled. As our dear friend, Hal Lewis, used to say, "Nothing works in the face of stupidity." It is vital that every rule and regulation in the school be logical, defensible and intelligently administered.

As Holloway (2002), Skiba and Peterson (1999), and others have pointed out, adhering blindly to a zero-tolerance school policy that denies students their fundamental rights to education is morally unjust, democratically offensive, and exacerbates problems. Holloway argued that school officials should evaluate each student's behavior on an individual, case-by-case basis. This fits perfectly with the democratic spirit of the Six-C Process.

Targeted Objective

Remind yourself often of your objective of the conflict—to resolve a concern—and focus squarely on it. Do not be drawn off the primary objective by being distracted by counterconcerns, incidental objectives, or secondary problems. Keep in mind what you want, and stick to it. To illustrate the power of a targeted objective, consider the action of Cato, the Roman statesman.

> In the year 149 BC, Cato was convinced that Rome would never be secure while the great city of Carthage on the North African coast remained its rival. Whenever called upon to speak in the Roman Senate, whatever the subject under debate, Cato always concluded his remarks with "Carthago delenda est" (Carthage must be destroyed!). Through his targeted objective and perseverance, Cato was able to instigate the third Punic War, and Carthage was totally destroyed.

When individuals work to move from conflict to conciliation, they will do well by keeping the SUNSET model in mind. The Naval War College formula of 02S4MEC contributed to the historic U.S. naval victory at the Battle of Midway during World War II. Perhaps SUNSET will assist you in managing combat situations in a satisfactory manner.

TAKING A STAND

Now that you have made a decision to address a significant concern at the combat level, the final step is to find the courage to act. This action often involves the administration of some sort of penalty. In Chapter 5, we presented such penalties as natural or logical consequences. Although Dreikurs (1968) was one of the first theorists to write about using logical consequences as the result of inappropriate or irresponsible behaviors, many other contemporary educators and theorists, such as William Glasser (1998), have presented logical consequences as constructive, positive, and successful alternatives to brute punishment.

To apply logical consequences at the combat level, it is vital to convey to all participants involved with the concern that you have no personal bias or prejudice in using your authority to take appropriate action. At the same time, the most appropriate logical consequences have an element of agreement involved in their selection and application. For example, in a classroom discussion at the beginning of the year, students might agree that failure to complete desk assignments will result in a loss of recess time or require after school make-up work. The availability of choices helps make logical consequences more palatable and useful in responding to ill-advised behavior.

Key Point 6.7

When using logical consequences at the combat level, it is vital to convey to all participants involved with the concern that you have no personal bias or prejudice in using your authority to take appropriate action.

Here are some practical suggestions when applying logical consequences:

- Implement the chosen consequence calmly, with care and respect, and without punitive intent.
- Connect the consequence with the concern.
- Be certain that the person receiving the consequence has been previously informed of it and understands the specific concern (e.g., misbehavior).
- Emphasize the value of changing the situation (concern) rather than the negative aspects of the consequence.
- Focus on the choices available.
- Limit long explanations or arguments.

All of these behaviors are anchored in respect.

CIVILIZED DISSENT

Another word of caution seems appropriate. You do not design or apply logical consequences to stifle civilized dissent or encourage authoritarianism. As Kingsweel (1994), Forni (2008), and others have pointed out, civility is more than polite behavior and good manners. It is also basic orientation to social interaction. Civility demands openness to the claims of others, combined with willing restraint of one's own claims in the service of our common social projects. Civilized disagreement is one of the valued attributes of a democratic society. Civility provides us with the most democratic and civilized cohesion that we are likely to find. It ensures that society recognizes and values responsibilities while keeping personal desires and needs under reasonable control.

Key Point 6.8

The goal is to combat a troublesome situation, not go to war. Still, civilized conflict is a valued attribute of a democratic society.

Civilized dissent also disclaims and precludes physical violence whenever possible. An example here might be useful.

Some decades ago, an American visiting China was observing some Chinese laborers at a Shanghai waterfront carrying their heavy burdens. Two of the workers became engaged in a fierce argument. They rapidly exchanged what seemed to be hostile words. Fists were clinched and anger filled the air. It appeared that a physical fight was about to happen. The American waited, expecting a fight, but neither contestant threw a punch. After waiting a few minutes with nothing happening except a fierce verbal quarrel, the American turned to a Chinese friend and asked when the fistfight would begin. "Oh," replied the Chinese, smiling, "I cannot say. You see, the man who strikes the first blow admits that he has run out of ideas."

Words offer the most civilized, human, and nonviolent resolution to conflicts.

Key Point 6.9

Civility is more than polite behavior and good manners. It is also basic orientation to social interaction. Civility demands openness to the claims of others.

In order not to run out of ideas on ways to successfully handle a combative situation, you will be wise to maintain a consistent stance in accordance with the Six-C Process: that people are able, valuable, and responsible and should be treated accordingly. Even in the midst of combat, behaviors that intentionally humiliate, ridicule, demean, or otherwise hurt someone may be wrong even if these behaviors result in resolving the troublesome situation. When the most severe penalties must be leveled, it is essential that the action be couched in respect and even sadness. Another story from history illustrates the concept of respect and sadness.

> *At the end of a great naval battle of World War II, when British sailors were crowded on the decks of their ship, cheering the final death struggle of the great German battleship,* Bismarck, *a British Naval Officer reminded his men, "Don't cheer, men. Those poor souls are dying."*

Never lose your respect for others when you decide to combat a concern. Another real-life story shared by a school principal illustrates the value of compassion, even in a combat situation.

> *The young principal had to terminate a highly successful teacher because of her repeated use of alcohol at work. In his office, the terminated teacher broke down and sobbed uncontrollably. This hurt the principal very much. He phoned a more experienced principal for advice on what he could have done in this situation. The older principal replied, "You could cry with her, and then do everything possible to find her some help for her addiction."*

The two previous examples illustrate that when combat is necessary and penalties are inevitable, it is understandable to experience sadness. As a final reminder, respect remains an essential ingredient in the process, so you can grieve and show compassion when the combat ends. This is especially important to remember as we move to the sixth and final level in the Six-C Process: conciliate.

Key Point 6.10

When you must apply the most severe penalties, it is essential that your actions be couched in respect and even sadness.

SUMMARY

This chapter presented the fifth C of the Six-C Process, *combat*. It stressed that the combat is with a specific situation and not with individuals or groups of people. Like the preceding chapters, caution was emphasized in moving toward more serious and demanding levels to address your original concern. The acronym SUNSET was presented as a means to combat a difficult and challenging situation in the most humane and effective manner. Combat requires courage and a willingness to take a stand. It involves allowing natural and logical consequences to take their course. The next chapter introduces what is perhaps the most important C in the Six-C Process—*conciliation*.

Major Themes

- Combat is a most serious level of intervention when dealing with your concerns. Yet, when done with civility, respect, and fairness, combat can help you resolve problem situations with desired outcomes.

- Even when you apply the most judicious use of respectful and logical consequences, some individuals may still resist these actions and perceive them as harsh punishments. Acquiring this understanding is key to becoming consistent when you move into a combat situation.
- Similar to the use of penalties in combat, you use power with deliberate discretion. Understand the authority you have to use, particularly leverage and control, in combat situations; and be cognizant of the power available to others involved in each circumstance. Everyone has some level and type of power at their disposal.
- As with other levels of the Six-C Process, having a mental structure or mnemonic device can assist you in combating situations. In this chapter, the acronym SUNSET provided six points of reference to help you through combat.
- When combating problem situations, be aware of the value of civilized dissent in democratic societies, including schools. Differentiating between civilized dissent and anarchy is important in the process of deciding whether to go to combat.

CHAPTER SEVEN

Conciliation and Beyond

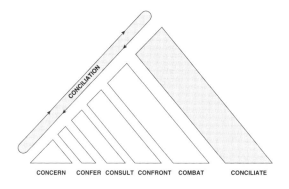

A newly appointed high school English teacher suspects that a student has plagiarized his theme paper. The teacher thinks it is too well written for a high school student. In a conference with him, the teacher shares her suspicion, but the student insists that the paper is his own work. The teacher escalates the action to combat level by threatening to give him an F for the paper. The student storms out of the classroom yelling that the teacher is ignorant and grossly "Unfair!" In checking with other teachers, the new teacher gathers information that contradicts her suspicion about plagiarism. The teachers share with their new colleague some excellent

(Continued)

(Continued)

papers written by the student in question, and support his contention that his work is original. Indeed, he is a talented writer. Embarrassed, the English teacher goes to the student and apologizes, but the student, still hurting from the false accusation, rejects her act of contrition. What might the teacher do at this point?

To conciliate is to unite, usually in a spirit of goodwill. In the Six-C Process, *conciliate* means to reach out for some sort of agreement, mutual trust, and shared respect, with the aim of starting afresh. Finding a solution to a particular concern is usually insufficient. As emphasized earlier in this book, if the stress caused by the previous levels of the Six-C Process is not addressed, the stress may extend far beyond the original concern. Working through conflict is as much a healing process as it is a resolution product.

A brief example might be useful. Lawyers who follow ethical standards seek to consider the welfare of everyone involved in legal disputes. At the end of a bitter divorce settlement, an angry husband wanted to reveal some very hurtful information about his wife. His attorney asked him, "Is it really in your best interest to humiliate your wife in front of your children?" Upon reflection, the husband decided to let bygones be bygones and the healing process begin.

The idea that people can come together in caring, thoughtful, and creative ways to deal with conflicts sounds easy, perhaps too easy. In practice, combating a conflict-ridden situation is often difficult, disruptive, and dreaded. Fortunately, the Six-C Process provides a rationale for and examples of caring, thoughtful, and creative practices.

Can you guarantee that all difficulties, disruptions, and dreaded experiences will go away if the Six-C Process is followed? Certainly not, but many conflicts can be ameliorated. That is, bad situations can be made less bad and good situations can be made better if the spirit of the Six-C Process is taken to heart, intelligently considered, and intentionally put into practice. For this to happen, you will find it valuable to incorporate careful thought and effort into the last C, conciliation.

Key Point 7.1

You can make conflicts less difficult if you take the spirit of the Six-C Process to heart, consider it intelligently, and intentionally put it into practice.

Conciliate means to bring together, to unite after a period of separation. Although this is especially important if the combat stage has been reached, it is also necessary after each of the other four levels (concern, confer, consult, and confront) to restore a working stability and openness to new possibilities.

On an international level, the concept of conciliation was vital in the peaceful developments in South Africa after the end of the policy of racial apartheid. An unjust system had been successfully combated in 1994, and there was the strong possibility that violence and instability could beset the rapidly changing nation. To provide social stability and a new unity, the Truth and Reconciliation Commission was established in 1995 to deal with human rights violations that occurred during the apartheid era. The commission went around the country and was empowered to grant amnesty, within certain constraints, and to disclose politically motivated crimes by combatants on all sides.

Although there are those who were critical of the results, most would agree that what could have been an ongoing escalation of horrific events had been ameliorated (Chapman & van der Merwe, 2007). The visionary and brilliant foresight of Nelson Mandela, Desmond Tutu, and others to seek unity after terrible conflict has been a model to countries around the world. To seek conciliation as a creative alternative to continued violence or seething silence is now seen as an important step after conflicts within and between nations. Implacable enemies can become strong allies, as witnessed when Germany, Italy, and Japan became allies of the United States, England, and other countries they battled in World War II.

The personal power of conciliation was experienced by one of the authors a few years ago. It still has his head spinning.

> At a school reunion, he happened to spot an older classmate who bullied him when he was in junior high school. Over the years, he thought about this bully and had visions of confronting him at such an event some time in the future. Well, when the time came, some 45 years later, the author was a bit hesitant. He thought, "What if this turns into a heated discussion? What if we reach the combat stage in public? What if this turns really ugly?" These were not pretty thoughts. But then, he thought, "What if I approach this in a milder manner? What if I am low-key in our discussion?" His second, reflected thoughts won out. At the reunion, he approached his former schoolmate and introduced himself. To his surprise, his classmate exuded enthusiasm in seeing him. This went on for a few minutes until the author decided to ask him the pointed question, "Did you hate me in junior high school?" His former schoolmate stopped for a second, took a deep breath, and said, "I hated everyone then." He took another breath and said, "I was being sexually abused by a neighbor at that time and was all messed up. For many years, I went to therapy to get myself together. I think I have done that. I am really sorry for all the pain I caused people then, and I've really changed my life." They then talked for a few minutes, hugged, and said goodbye. Now, they never became good friends or even had a chance to talk after that, but there was a peaceful and insightful coming together after a bad relationship, and they left the encounter with a feeling of mutual respect. For the author, old wounds and anticipated retaliation were healed by the genuine experience of conciliation.

CONCILIATION AFTER COMBAT

Combating a conflicting situation, no matter how humane and thoughtful the efforts, can still leave a feeling of ambiguity, discomfort, and hostility on the combatants and noncombatants. This is why it is necessary to go beyond combat to conciliation to make serious attempts at determining what has happened and to reunite in a deeper, more respectful way.

We wish that reaching conciliation would always work out as smoothly as it did for a friend of one of the authors, a high school science teacher.

Some years earlier, this teacher was conducting a science class during summer school and one student did not complete the required assignments. This was a rare experience for this teacher, who took pride in his ability to work with difficult students. Even though he tried several times and in various ways to have the student finish his work, the teacher was unsuccessful. The student did not get credit for the course.

Years later, the teacher was playing miniature golf with a group of people when the former student, who was drinking heavily, spotted him. The student came toward his former teacher in an in-your-face manner and said, "Hey, you're the guy who failed me in science." The teacher turned to the student and looked at him in a caring but firm way, greeted him by name, and then waited. Surprisingly, the student stopped, just nodded, and walked away saying, "I know, I know, I know, I failed myself." After a few minutes, the teacher smiled and said to the group, "You know, it doesn't always go that way."

Key Point 7.2

Going beyond combat to conciliation makes a serious attempt at determining what has happened and continuing the relationship in a deeper, more respectful way.

As noted earlier, even the most humane and well-intended combat can leave a residue of uncertainty, uneasiness, and unfriendliness in relationships. With this in mind, there are six basic rules to consider after combating the situation:

1. Let the fire die down

2. Give people space and time

3. Use intermediaries

4. Let bygones be bygones

5. Trust the process

6. Be willing to make amends

Each rule requires some elaboration.

1. Let the Fire Die Down

After combating a difficult situation in a firm and humane way, there is often some resentment and hostility that remains. For example, if a student did not pass a course and is repeating it with you, feeling a lot of anger and resentment, there is a tendency to want to let that student know that his or her inattention, bad attitude, or careless work habits need to be changed. As tempting as it is to sermonize about this, it often has the effects of throwing gasoline on the fire.

In the previous story of the science teacher and former student, imagine what would have happened if the teacher had gotten back in the student's face and said "No, you failed yourself!" Most likely, the student would have been defensive and even more belligerent. By using indirect modes of action, you may get behavioral changes without the emotional heat. Indirect modes of action, as shown above, involve remaining calm, letting the other person know you have heard what they have said and meant, and expressing your point of view in a respectful manner. This respect may require time and space.

2. Give People Space and Time

Sometimes when things have gone wrong, people need time to come to grips with what has happened and redefine who they are and how they want to be. An overly enthusiastic attempt to get someone back on a horse after being thrown can be too much, too soon. Their memory of the horse might be that of a bucking bronco.

Giving people some space and time to settle back in and get comfortable about what is going on is a sign of respect and acknowledgment of the complex ways feelings operate in our lives. One of the authors came to a late realization of this when talking to his daughter.

> *As an energetic educator, he liked to deal with conflicts as learning experiences for both parties. Often after a long discussion with his daughter in which they eventually reached some agreement, he would tell her what he learned about himself during their disagreement and wanted her to do the same. Bad idea. This was too much, too soon. What she needed (and*

probably him too) was to be left alone for a while and let the thoughts and feelings that were running rampant slow down. This was not the time to try to logically follow a train of thought when tense emotions were occurring. Interestingly, what the author found out is that often his daughter, given some time and space, would internalize some of the key values and phrases they considered and would insert them in discussions with her friends.

An illustration of the value of letting time be the healer was provided by Lopez-Morillas (Pupo-Walker, Lopez-Morillas, & Cabeza de Vaca, 1993) in his translations of accounts written by early Spanish conquistadors of the cultures they encountered in the New World. The conquistadors described the healing practice of one culture this way:

And when in some aboriginal villages there are those who quarrel and have disputes among themselves, they strike and beat each other to the point of exhaustion and then draw apart. After they had pummeled each other, they take their houses and their wives and go live in the plains, away from the others, until their anger has cooled. And when they have overcome their animosity and are no longer angry, they return to their village and from then on are friends, as though nothing had happened between them, nor does anyone have to make peace between them, for this is the way they settle their quarrels. (pp. 79–80)

3. Use Intermediaries

Sometimes, the best person to talk to the other party is anyone other than you. In the formal process of conciliation, a conciliator will work separately with each party. Often, people will share feelings with a third party that they prefer not to share with each other. This is the reason some marriage counselors prefer to work with each partner separately before working with them together. By getting to know each partner separately, the marriage counselor is in a stronger position to bring conciliation when the couple is together for a session. In schools, a counselor, another teacher, an administrator, or one or more students can take this role as conciliator.

Key Point 7.3

After combating a difficult situation, it is often helpful to have someone else work with the combatants.

The power of intermediaries can easily be seen among families and friends. Parents mediate between siblings, children mediate between their parents, and friends mediate between friends. For example, when one child accidentally runs into another child and knocks him down, it is not unusual to see a third child help the fallen child off the ground and say, "He didn't mean to run into you."

One of the key things that the intermediary can do is to communicate *double-strength* invitations, positive things that each person has said about the other. They are called *double-strength* because they come through a third party. In addition, intermediaries can keep participants better informed and on task with what may be happening in families, classrooms, schools, or the larger community.

4. Let Bygones Be Bygones

Whenever possible, remember to forget and forget to remember. A beautiful example of letting go of negative feelings was provided by the actions of Edith Cavell. Cavell was a Red Cross nurse during World War I.

> During her service in Belgium, she helped Allied soldiers to escape from behind German lines. Cavell was captured by the Germans, and sentenced to death. As she was led before the firing squad, she is reported to have said, "I realize that patriotism is not enough. I must have no hatred or bitterness towards anyone." (Bartlett, 1992, p. 590)

Such noble sentiments are beyond the reach of most of us, but they serve as a powerful reminder of what is possible in the human spirit.

Key Point 7.4

Whenever possible, remember to forget, and forget to remember.
After a conflict, start out with a clean slate.

After a conflict, start out with a clean slate. For example, suppose you are teaching high school, and in front of the entire class, an angry student gives you the infamous finger. It produces a lot of student laughter in the class. It also produces a week's suspension from school. When the student returns to the classroom, it is essential that you do not hold a grudge. The student misbehaved and suffered logical consequences. Now is the time for a new beginning, a fresh start. What is done is done. Nothing can change the past; so look ahead.

5. Trust the Process

Although it is important to forget angry and disruptive thoughts after a conflict ends, it is equally vital to retain the principles and strategies of the Six-C Process. Understandably, after the combat level has ended, there may remain feelings of frustration and resentment. These feelings zap your energy, adding to the exhaustion that often follows a combat situation. In counteracting this depletion of energy and sense of vulnerability, you will want to avoid knee-jerk, get tough, "my way or the highway," and in-your-face behaviors and policies. Such thoughts and actions have no part to play in the Six-C Process.

Key Point 7.5

To make conciliation work, it is important to apply conciliatory
practices after each C in the Six-C Process.

---

6. Be Willing to Make Amends

There will be times when the evidence confirms that you have wronged another person. Be quick to make amends for this transgression. A sincere apology may be the first step. Some people think that apologizing is a sign of weakness or subservience. On the contrary, acknowledging that you have made a mistake, having the courage to apologize, and seeking to make amends are signs of strength.

Apologizing involves regret and sorrow. Regret expresses a feeling of disappointment about a situation. Sorrow is an expression of sadness about an event. Both are important feelings to convey when you have made a mistake that has done harm or in some way hurt another person. However, beyond regret and sorrow, an apology is taking responsibility for your actions and admitting a wrongdoing. In addition, an apology is an expression of contriteness, which includes a sense of restitution or restoration. Regret, sorrow, and contriteness are unlikely to mend relationships unless you address the actions that contributed to the situation and make amends for the damage or hurt they caused. Some illustrations might highlight the difference among regret, sorrow, contriteness, and making amends.

> Suppose that you have unjustly accused a student of being a gang member simply because she wears a black leather jacket to school. Later, you discover that you have seriously misjudged the student, and accused her falsely. One appropriate response would be to say, "I regret that I unjustly accused you of being in a gang." Such expression of regret might seem sufficient, yet it does not involve responsibility or penitence. Similarly, the response, "I am sorry about my accusation. I was wrong," is strong but does not move the relationship forward. Moving beyond regret and sorrow, you acknowledge your mistake, ask how you might make it up to the student, and express genuine contrition for a grievous act.

Expressing genuine contrition is more than what we often see in today's media, where people try to escape punishment for their misdeeds. Any apology is stripped of its healing power when it is insincere, stiff, or based primarily on self-interest. Moreover, coerced apologies are meaningless. A sincere apology sets the stage for what zoologists call a "reconciliation protocol." This is when animals seek to make up for their misbehavior.

There is further advantage for expressing sincere regret. Nancy Gibbs (2009), in an essay for *Time* magazine, reported that most people file lawsuits out of anger, not greed. Medical person-nel who express sincere sorrow when something goes awry are less likely to be sued. Following sincere apologies, the number of medical malpractice suits are significantly reduced. The same is true of hospitals, where malpractice suits have been known to drop by half. Your next step in the conciliatory process is to make amends and learn from your erroneous behavior.

You have the responsibility to make amends for your misdeeds in whatever way possible. As an old adage teaches, if you owe someone money, and God forgives you, that still does not repay the debt. For example, if you falsely accuse a student of something, you might seek to make amends by contacting everyone involved and writing a personal and public apology for your error. Apologizing to someone in private for hurtful things said in public is unlikely to make full amends. On the other hand, public action may well con-tribute to the healing process. To illustrate, a disturbing event took place while the U.S. President was presenting to a joint session of Congress. During the speech, a congressman shouted, "You Lie!" Later the congressman apologized to the President in private, but refused to apologize in public. This is insufficient. When you insult someone publicly, you want to apologize publicly.

In addition to doing everything you can to rectify your mistake, it is essential to make a personal commitment that you will seek to avoid similar mistakes in the future. Remember the question raised in Chapter 2, "Is your concern due to personal prejudices or biases?" Monitoring your suppositions and avoiding stereotypical thinking, you minimize the types of mistakes made in the above illustration.

In using all the above basic rules of the Six-C Process for concil-iation after combat, we once again emphasize the importance of the concept "lower is better." The principle of handling conflicts at the lowest level of intensity is probably most important during times of potential hostility and acrimony. Ironically, this is when conciliation is most difficult. To make conciliation work after com-bat, it is important to apply conciliatory practices after each C in the Six C Process, as suggested by the drawing in Chapter 1 (see Diagram 1.1).

CONCILIATION AS A REFLECTIVE PROCESS

Conciliation is a unique, uniting process. It is different from each of the other five Cs (concern, confer, consult, confront, and combat) in the Six-C Process in that each of the previous levels involves an increase of intensity and a focus on isolating the point of contention. Conciliation, on the other hand, requires a decrease in intensity. It is time to step back from a situation in an attempt to reconstruct a deeper and more meaningful unity. This is a time to learn important things about yourself and the world and to live more insightfully as a result of dealing with conflicting situations.

The following sections connect the process of conciliation with each of the previous C levels, beginning with Concern.

Conciliation and Concern

A key component of the first level of the Six-C Process requires that you make a decision on whether an issue is a concern or a preference. Understanding and living this distinction is important because it can free you from believing that decisive action needs to be taken every time you have a concern. It is a liberating feeling and an important part of your psychological health not to be concerned about everything all the time. The world can, and does, turn without us. Even though you may know this on a rational level, there is a tendency to feel guilty for inaction if the distinction between a concern and preference is not intentionally brought to light. In fact, worrying about taking responsibility for everything can be energy depleting and make it difficult to provide intentional caring action when and where it is really needed.

Once you have decided that your concern is more than a preference, your next decision is to determine whether the concern is *latent* or *actionable*, two concepts we introduced earlier in this book. If the concern is latent, it does not require your measured action, but it may bear watching. If the concern is actionable, it deserves your immediate attention. For example, if a colleague leaves a mess in the faculty workroom once or twice, this might be a latent concern. If the same colleague continues to leave the workroom in disarray, then it becomes an actionable concern for you and perhaps other faculty members. This is a good time to apply the 3+++wish? explained in Chapter 3.

In earlier chapters, we emphasized the impact of intentional reframing and how it guides your actions. Research evidence (Hockaday, Purkey, & Davis, 2001) suggests that by purposely reframing general thoughts into clearly stated, self-talk, you are in a much better position to accomplish your goals and are more likely to do so. The more clearly stated is your self-talk, the more likely your inner dialogue will result in positive action. For example, if you *say* to yourself, " I need to go to the bank," you are more likely to act upon that message than if you merely *think* about stopping by the bank. By *speaking* to yourself internally in clear language, and *listening* to this covert self-talk, you are more likely to respond overtly in the desired manner. Subsequently, you will more likely be reasonable with yourself about your responsibilities.

Returning to the concept of taking reasonable responsibility, seeing an issue as a preference rather than a concern does not mean abdication of your feelings about what is occurring. Rather, it means developing a positive and realistic view of yourself and others so that appropriate action can be taken when necessary.

Since time is a diminishing and nonrenewable resource, putting it to good use is a sign of living a healthy psychological and educationally productive life. As our colleague, Betty Siegel, has pointed out, we are all juggling balls. Some are rubber and some are glass. The rubber ones will bounce back, but the glass ones, the truly significant things in our lives, might break if we drop them. We have to make sure we do not drop the ones that really matter. The conciliation process at this level means deciding what is realistic and responsible in order to have the energy to focus on what really matters.

Conciliation and Confer

At the confer level of the Six-C Process, you decide that there is a professional, moral, or personal issue that needs to be addressed in a caring manner, perhaps by using the 3+++wish? formula. The conciliation component here involves dealing with your integrity and vulnerability. Integrity is involved because it is essential that the three pluses you communicate are genuine and meaningful. This means looking for positive and real qualities in the person with whom you have a concern. This therapeutic authenticity, the intention to be honest and above board about our relationship and purpose, is not always easy, but it is always required (Patterson, 1984). Conciliation involves rethinking what you believe about what you can and will do in terms of affirming others.

Conciliation also means determining your vulnerability in using the 3+++wish? statement, "Will you do this for me?" To ask someone to do something for you is a sign that you want to enter a more personal relationship. This involves risks and responsibilities. People can reject you, let you down, or ask a favor of you in return. It is much safer to avoid relationships and commitments, but this comes with the dangers of isolation and loneliness.

One of the authors had a difficult time asking people, "Will you do this for me?" He likes to see himself as very independent and others as having to make unencumbered choices for themselves. However, upon reflection, it occurred to him that not only is he independent, but he is also interdependent, connected to others in caring ways. In addition, he likes doing things for others. Therefore, not asking them to do things for him deprives them of the pleasure of providing assistance. It also deprives you of providing service to others. By not ever asking for help, it discourages others from asking help of you. The conciliation process related to confer involves constructing a more integrated and courageous self.

Conciliation and Consult

During the consult level of the Six-C Process, you remind the other person that the concern is not resolved. This is particularly troublesome when the other person has tacitly given his or her word by responding affirmatively to the original request. In addition, you undertake a deeper examination of possible actions. Conciliation here begins with the issue of reminding someone of a troublesome and continuing concern. This is often difficult to do, especially if you have a personal relationship with the other person. It is often easier to overlook what was promised but not delivered and to pretend everything is fine. Here, however, doing the easier thing often leads to bigger problems. Accepting irresponsible behavior undermines the quality of a relationship and the integrity of the institution in which you are working.

One of the authors became chair of his department and realized that he would have to remind and, at times, nudge others to get things done. He found that in approaching difficult situations, the phrase, "I would be remiss in my responsibilities as chair if I did not (mention the particular action or infraction)" enabled him to begin necessary discussions. This wording communicated that he took his responsibilities seriously, and it was not a personal issue. It also followed the consultative structure presented in

Chapter 4. Conciliation involves finding the words that can unify your intentions and get you going in the right direction.

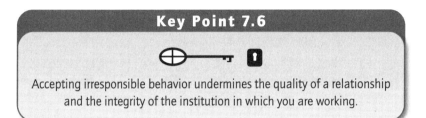

Key Point 7.6

Accepting irresponsible behavior undermines the quality of a relationship and the integrity of the institution in which you are working.

Since problem solving is an important part of the consult level, seeing yourself as a problem solver is essential. Similar to the scientific method, problem solving involves compiling and considering information, inquiry, and ingenuity. The conciliation process here is the ability to work with others in an open and honest way to develop a plan for resolving a difficulty. Achieving this unification of purpose and product means an honest evaluation of possibilities and impossibilities. When this is done well, a deeper feeling of respect can develop.

Conciliation and Confront

Often, at the confront level, frustration sets in. You have worked hard, become vulnerable, perhaps even been betrayed, and you are in an even deeper conflict. It seems so unfair. The tendency here is to throw in the towel (retreat) or retaliate (aggress). Conciliation, however, does not work that way. To paraphrase an old saying, when the going gets tough, the conciliation gets going. At this level, conciliation means learning to see yourself as a caring and determined person who is willing to face an issue squarely.

Determining and stating realistic consequences moves interactions from mutual problem solving to stipulation of consequences. It is not for the faint of heart. What is reconciled at this stage is the ability to be both empathic and firm, to care for others, yourself, and your personal and professional responsibilities.

Seeking to unify complex and competing responsibilities is not easy, but it is necessary for becoming what Neiman (2008) called grown-up idealists. Grown-up idealists are people who realize that even though they are not perfect, they are required to face up to their responsibilities. Confronting others with consequences for their actions—even though you are imperfect yourself—is to develop a more complex self. This more complex self is capable of more nuanced and dependable behavior in an often-tumultuous world.

Key Point 7.7

Conciliation means coming to terms with yourself as a caring and determined person who is willing to face an issue squarely.

Conciliation and Combat

To combat a situation is to realize that you will not remain passive when it is necessary to take action that prevents a greater wrong from occurring. If a concern has not gone away and you have taken empathic and thoughtful steps, then not to follow up on a warning is to negate your sense of fairness and responsibility. Coming to this level requires patience and wisdom. Withholding consequential action until all other avenues have been exhausted requires noteworthy patience. Knowing when and how to take action necessitates compassionate wisdom. Unifying the two leads to the development of wise patience, the ability to take the right action at the right time in the right way, along with patient wisdom, the ability to avoid imposing premature judgments.

Fortunately, if the conciliatory spirit of the Six-C Process is followed, reflected patience and wisdom will tend to develop as new complexities occur. Reflection on conciliation at each phase of the Six-C Process is an educational, empathic, and energetic way to deepen that possibility and take it beyond the sixth C.

BEYOND CONCILIATION

The Six-C Process can work with many diverse groups and with myriad types of conflicts. Your focus in using the Six Cs is to have the behavior of others change when they are doing something that is dangerous, irresponsible, immoral, illegal, or flat-out annoying. This covers many but not all conflict situations. Your personal and professional life would be easier and more productive if you worked through such conflicts in caring and efficient ways. However, in a world that has been described as pluralistic and postmodern, there are, by definition, a wide variety of conflicting philosophical perspectives and no consensual trump card to reconcile these differences.

Philosophical Differences

Philosophical differences, differences of value and perspective, run deep and the conflicts they engender touch all aspects of life. What is a caring, conscientious, committed educator or helping professional to do? Following the advice of Dale Carnegie (1936), if people want to win friends and influence people, they should refrain from talking about politics, religion, or heat-generating topics. This is good advice some of the time. Avoiding uncomfortable topics has its place. At times, the phrases "Don't go there" or "Too much information" can serve a useful purpose and let someone know that this is not the appropriate time to discuss certain things. However, a dedicated, sustained silence on philosophical conflicts would leave us all isolated and impoverished.

A democratic society, an educative society, is built on the necessity of people with deep-seated differences being able to discuss issues of mutual importance and to grow in the process. The job of those who cherish the democratic ideal is to keep this spirit alive through reflection, dialogue, and ethical practice. Educators and helping professionals committed to a democratic society need to model ways for such deep discussions to happen.

Key Point 7.8

A democratic society, an educative society, is built on the necessity of people with deep-seated differences being able to discuss issues of mutual importance and to grow in the process.

SPURT-Q Method

One approach to philosophical conflicts, developed by one of the authors, is the *SPURT-Q method*. An incipient form of the SPURT-Q method began in a philosophical conversation between one of the authors and his then 11-year-old daughter.

> While on ski lifts, the father and daughter engaged in some of their best conversations. This time, the father told his daughter about the ideas of continuity and interaction. He explained that if you take this idea seriously then you realize that everything that ever happened in the universe has led up to this moment, and consequently, what we do now will influence the rest of the universe. He was surprised by his daughter's silence after his statement and waited to see if she was going to respond. After a few moments, she said one word, "Perhaps," and then was silent again. After a few moments she then added, "Upon reflection, we can all get sucked into a black hole and so it won't really matter at all." Her father was then silent and actually stunned for a few seconds, and then finally said, "Perhaps, but it matters now and that should count for something."

The author is still amazed at the style of thought and choice of words his daughter used. Today many years later, they continue this philosophical discussion. Healthy and productive philosophical conversations can get deeper, more interesting, and bring people closer together.

The basic framework of that conversation was the foundation for a way to discuss philosophical issues that can be of service for the development of a deeper democratic society. Such philosophical discussion

- Shows respect for the other person;
- Demonstrates that you take seriously what the other person has proposed;
- Provides positive common ground for furthering the conversation;
- Allows you to ask an important question about what has been said; and
- Invites the possibility for mutually exploring the issue.

These points led to the development of the SPURT-Q method. Each symbol stands for an important step in the process.

The SPURT-Q Method

S: Silence and time to thoughtfully think it over

P: Perhaps—you experience feelings of disagreement, agreement, and perplexity

UR: Upon reflection, you are able to articulate your reaction

T: Tentative agreement—you search for common ground

Q: Question—you ask to extend the conversation

1. S—Silence. Silence can be golden, at least at the beginning of a philosophic discussion. Thoughtful philosophical statements require more than knee-jerk responses. They require some time to take in and think seriously about what has been said. Often, to respond immediately to what the other person has said with an off-the-cuff remark is to miss the subtlety or seriousness involved in the statement and to communicate that the person's statement is really not worth taking the time or effort to think about.

Legend has it that when John Dewey, one of the 20th century's leading philosophers, was teaching at Columbia and was asked a philosophical question, he would often remain silent for three to five minutes and then provide a detailed and carefully considered response. Dewey took seriously thoughtful philosophical questions. His response time may be too long for most conversations now— and even then—but silence can be a key element in developing more complex thoughts on difficult issues.

2. P—Perhaps. *Perhaps* could be the most important word in a philosophical conversation. All too often, people use *perhaps* to mean *whatever* and dismiss what has been said. It does not have to be a dismissive term. When used honestly and without sarcasm, the word *perhaps* means that regarding what has been said, there is something that you agree with and something you have questions about. Using the word *perhaps* means that you want to hear more and there is more to talk about.

3. UR—Upon Reflection. Saying, "Upon reflection" means that you have given the comment some serious thought and want

the conversation to continue. This phrase signals that you wish to go beyond superficial comments and move to a deeper level of discourse. In this book, you have learned about the value of reflective thinking when applying the Six-C Process. It is especially important in philosophical discussions.

4. T—Tentative Agreement. As stated earlier, the word *perhaps* implies that there is something that you agreed with in what another person said. The T indicates what part of the other person's statement you agree with by restating or reinterpreting it. Surprisingly, very seldom do people make comments that we find totally objectionable. Usually, we can locate or unearth something we can agree with either in terms of content or intent. This serves as common ground for furthering the conversation. It gets us out of the debater's mindset and into a dialogical mode—the seeking of a deeper common ground amidst important differences.

5. Q—Question. Going back again to the sincere use of the word *perhaps*, it also implies that we are not in total agreement with what the other person has said. The question part of the method is the time to raise an important concern or query you have about what has been said. It is important that the question be a genuine puzzlement or clarification. Merely playing the devil's advocate or trying to get another's goat does a disservice to genuine dialogue. The sincere question raised then becomes the springboard for a mutual search for more complex principles to accommodate the complexities and subtleties that emerge.

Key Point 7.9

When used honestly, the word *perhaps* means that, regarding what the person has said, there is something that you agree with and something you have questions about.

This is what the SPURT-Q looks like in the abstract. Now, let us see what it might look like in the concrete.

Imagine that a colleague makes a comment with which you really want to take issue. For example, suppose your colleague says,

"Students these days really have it too easy." You can appreciate where your colleague is coming from, have some disagreement with this comment as first stated, and wish that your colleague could understand more of your sentiments on this issue. You realize that this is a preference rather than a concern. Nevertheless, you decide that rather than being silent, you will use the SPURT-Q method to invite a deeper conversation. Here is what the conversation might look like.

1. You are silent for at least three seconds and take in seriously what you perceive your colleague said and what he or she might have meant.

2. You say, "Perhaps," and sincerely mean it.

3. You give some thought as to why you said perhaps, and then you add, "Upon reflection."

4. You follow up the reflective phrase with the tentative agreement, "I can agree that students have many conveniences and opportunities that we did not have when we were their age, and in many ways I would like to have what they now may take for granted."

5. You then raise your question by saying, "Do you think, however, that the world they are living in is more dangerous, hazardous, and ambiguous?"

If things go well, this may lead to a more extended conversation on the nature of the advantages and disadvantages each generation lives with and how educators may address these issues.

Following are additional examples of the SPURT-Q method in action. They are idealized examples of ways to begin philosophical discussions. The intention of each is to deepen the ways you talk about complex issues that you encounter. Although agreement may not happen, a sounder understanding of issues and a more profound respect for each person can result. At at time when civility is missing from discussion of important social and philosophical issues, silence, reflection, agreement, and honest questions can extend the democratic discourse. You want to learn from and grow with each person in the conflicts you experience.

Example 1

A friend says, "We don't want a health care system like Canada's."

You are silent for at least three seconds.

You say, "Perhaps," and you mean it sincerely.

You give some thought about why you said perhaps, and continue, "Upon reflection, I can see how the Canadian health care system has been negatively portrayed as having many questionable aspects."

You ask your friend, "Do you think there may be other interpretations of the Canadian system?"

Example 2

A colleague says to you, "It is important to say what you believe regardless of the consequences."

You are silent for at least three seconds.

You say, "Perhaps" and mean it sincerely.

You give some thought about why you said perhaps, and continue, "Upon reflection, I agree that integrity is an important virtue."

You ask the colleague, "Do you think it matters how, when, and where you say what you believe?"

Example 3

A school administrator says, "We are going to have a zero-tolerance policy on bullying."

You are silent for at least three seconds.

You say, "Perhaps," and you mean it sincerely.

You give some thought to why you said perhaps, and continue, "Upon reflection, I agree that bullying is a serious issue in schools."

You ask the administrator, "What are some subtle forms of bullying that can be handled with a zero-tolerance policy?"

As mentioned, these are idealized views of conversations. All conversations regarding philosophical differences will not go this way. But some will. And that is progress. What the SPURT-Q method attempts to do is to turn two *nos* into a larger *yes* of mutual and honest exploration of a topic of worth to all involved. In a democratic society saturated with sound bites, sloganeering, spin, and the promise of instant gratification, deeper exploration of topics of mutual concern is sorely needed.

SUMMARY

This closing chapter looked at the final C in the Six-C Process: *conciliation*. As the concluding level in the process, conciliation is about unifying that which has been severed over a growing concern. Suggestions for bringing stability and growth were offered. In addition, this chapter presented conciliation as a necessary and reflective part of the other five levels. As such, each level has important elements that need unification after a conflict. Finally, the chapter ended by examining conflicts beyond the Six-C Process and offering the SPURT-Q method as a way to extend the dialogue about philosophical conflicts.

Perhaps, upon reflection, there is a seventh C that needs to be cultivated in a democratic society: *conversation*. We will leave the elaboration of that thought to another book at another time. In the meantime, should your time and energy permit, we would welcome the opportunity to converse with you about this book. We realize that many conflicts are deep seated and seem irresolvable. However, we also realize that in these conflicts there are also hidden opportunities that will be lost unless we enter the process with good will and imaginative acts of hope. In the words of Nelson Mandela, "It seems impossible until it's done." This book is done. We hope it makes better things possible, including future stimulating and surprising conversations. We would like to learn about your experiences with the Six-C Process, and we would welcome your ideas and suggestions. Please contact the lead author, Dr. William W. Purkey, at wwpurkey@aol.com.

Major Themes

- Conciliation is a part of the Six-C Process that has value for all the other levels. Although it is important as the closing level of the process, its attributes can facilitate implementation in all phases of conflict resolution.

- To conciliate after combat is particularly important because without a process of soothing wounds and making peace scars of battle will remain and sometimes reignite original or new concerns. Winning a particular battle is insufficient when you have a stake in continuing a healthy working, loving, or other relationship with the person or people involved.
- Use behaviors that have brought about a desirable outcome regarding your original concern and temper them with conciliatory behaviors, such as those mentioned in this chapter, to bring about opportunities for growth for you and all concerned.

References

Adler, A. (1954). *Understanding human nature* (W. B. Wolf, Trans.). New York: Fawcett Premier. (Original work published 1927)

Barlett, J. (1992). *Familiar quotations* (16th ed.). Boston: Little, Brown.

Berger, C. R., & Calabrese, R. J. (1975). Some explorations in initial interaction and beyond: Toward a developmental theory of interpersonal communication. *Human Communication Research, 1,* 99–112.

Bowen, B. (in press). Moving away from coercion: Enhancing patient dignity and respect. In M.R. Priviters (Ed.), *Workplace violence in the mental health and general health care system.* Boston: Jones and Bartlett.

Bowen, B., & Mohr, W. K. (2009). *Measuring the presence of coercion in psychiatric settings.* Proceedings of the 6th International Conference on Violence in Clinical Psychiatry, October 23–24. Stockholm, Sweden: Oud Consultancy.

Brown, D., Pryzwansky, W. B., & Schulte, A. C. (2006). *Psychological consultation and collaboration: Introduction to theory and practice.* Boston: Allyn & Bacon.

Burgess, G., & Burgess, H. (1996). *Constructive confrontation theoretical framework.* Retrieved September 3, 2009, from www.colorado.edu/conflict/hwltap7.htm

Burgess, G., & Burgess, H. (1997). *Constructive confrontation: A strategy for dealing with intractable environmental conflicts.* Retrieved September 3, 2009, from http://www.colorado.edu/conflict/full_text_search/AllCRCDocs/97-1.htm

Carnegie, D. (1936). *How to win friends and influence people.* New York: Simon & Schuster.

Chapman, A. R., & van der Merwe, H. (2007). *Truth and reconciliation in South Africa: Did the TRC deliver?* Philadelphia: University of Pennsylvania Press.

Combs, A. W., Avila, D. L., & Purkey, W. W. (1978). *Helping relationships: Basic concepts for the helping professions* (3rd ed.). Boston: Allyn & Bacon.

Combs, A. W., & Snygg, D. (1959). *Individual behavior: A perceptual approach to behavior* (2nd ed.). Boston: Harper & Row.

Dewey, J. (1916). *Democracy and education.* New York: Macmillan.

Dougherty, A. M. (2009). *Psychological consultation and collaboration in school and community settings.* Pacific Grove, CA: Brooks/Cole.

Dreikurs, R. (1968). *Psychology in the classroom* (2nd ed.). New York: Harper and Row.

Dreikurs, R., & Grey, L. (1968). *Logical consequences.* New York: Hawthorn Books.

Dryden, J., & Clough, A. H. (Eds.). (1977). *Plutarch's lives* (Rev. ed.). New York: Modern Library.

Egan, G. (2002). *The skilled helper* (7th ed.). Pacific Grove, CA: Brooks/Cole.

Fisher, R. (2005). *Beyond reason: Using emotions as you negotiate.* New York: Penguin.

Fisher, R., Ury, W., & Patton, B. (1991). *Getting to yes: Negotiating agreement without giving in* (2nd ed.). New York: Penguin Books.

Forni, P. M. (2008). *The civility solution: What to do when people are rude.* New York: St. Martin's.

Fullan, M. (2001). *Leading in a culture of change.* New York: Jossey-Bass.

George, R. L., & Cristiani, T. S. (1995). *Counseling: Theory and practice* (4th ed.). Boston: Allyn & Bacon.

Gibbs, N. (2009, March 30). The lost art of saying I am sorry. *Time, 173* (12), 72.

Gladding, S. T. (2009). *Counseling: A comprehensive profession* (6th ed.). Upper Saddle River, NJ: Merrill/Prentice Hall.

Gladwell, M. (2008). *Outliers: The story of success.* New York: Little, Brown.

Glasser, W. (1998). *Choice theory: A new psychology of personal freedom.* New York: HarperPerennial.

Gordon, T. (2000). *Parent effectiveness training: The proven program for raising responsible children.* New York: Three Rivers Press.

Gross, D. R., & Capuzzi, D. (2007). Helping relationships: From core dimensions to brief approaches. In D. Capuzzi and D. R. Goss (Eds.), *Counseling and psychotherapy: Theories and interventions* (4th ed., pp. 3–25). Upper Saddle River, NJ: Merrill/Prentice Hall.

Habermas, J. (1981). *The theory of communicative action* (Vol. 1). Cambridge, MA: Polity.

Hockaday, S., Purkey, W., & Davis, K. (2001, Fall). Intentionality in helping relationships: The influence of three forms of internal cognitions on behavior. *Journal of Humanistic Counseling, Education, and Development, 40,* 219–224.

Holloway, J. H. (2002). Research Line: The dilemma of zero tolerance. *Educational Leadership, 59*(4), 84–85.

Hoover, J., & DiSilvestro, R. P. (2005). *The art of constructive confrontation.* Hoboken, NJ: Wiley.

Jourard, S. M. (1964). *The transparent self: Self-disclosure and well-being.* Princeton, NJ: Van Nostrand.

Kidder, R. M. (1996). *How good people make tough choices: Resolving the dilemmas of ethical living.* New York: Fireside.

Kidder, R. (2005). *Moral courage.* New York: Harper Collins.

Kingsweel, M. (1994). Citizenship and civility: The true north strong and free, thank you. *University of Toronto Magazine, 22*(20), 14–19.

Kosmoski, G. J., & Pollack, D. R. (2001). *Managing conversations with hostile adults.* Thousand Oaks, CA: Corwin.

Kottler, J. (2008). *A brief primer of helping skills.* Thousand Oaks, CA: Sage.

Maslow, A. H. (1968). *Toward a psychology of being* (2nd ed.). Princeton, NJ: Van Nostrand.

Meier, S. T., & Davis, S. R. (1993). *The elements of counseling* (2nd ed.). Pacific Grove, CA: Brooks/Cole.

Neiman, S. (2008). *Moral clarity: A guide for grown-up idealists.* Orlando, FL: Harcourt.

Noddings, N. (1995, November). *Care and education.* Keynote address at the International Alliance for Invitational Education Conference, Greensboro, NC.

Novak, J. M. (2002). *Inviting educational leadership.* London: Pearson.

O'Flynn, S., & Kennedy, H. (2000). *Conflict and confrontation in the classroom.* Gortnaclough, Ireland: Paradigm.

Parsons, R. D., & Kahn, W. J. (2005). *The school counselor as consultant: An integrated model for school-based consultation.* Belmont, CA: Thompson-Brooks/Cole.

Patterson, C. H. (1984). Empathy, warmth and genuineness in psychotherapy: A review of reviews. *Psychotherapy, 21,* 431–438.

Pianta, R. (2008, January/February). Neither art nor accident. *Harvard Education Letter,* 1–3.

Podemski, R. S., & Childers, J. H., Jr. (1991). How to deal with angry people—Human relations strategies that work. *Journal of Educational Public Relations, 14*(3), 31.

Primary Prevention Committee of the Healthcare Coalition on Violence. (2003, October). *A review of research on corporal punishment.* Minneapolis, MN: Children's Hospitals and Clinics.

Pupo-Walker, E. Lopez-Morillas, F. M., & Cabeza de Vaca, A. N. (1993). *Castaways.* Berkeley: University of California Press.

Purkey, W. W. (1996, April). What the U.S. Naval War College can teach principals about school safety. *National Association of Secondary School Principals Bulletin,* 112–113.

Purkey, W. W. (2000). *What students say to themselves: Internal dialogue and school success.* Thousand Oaks, CA: Corwin.

Purkey, W. W. (2006). *Teaching class clowns (and what they can teach us).* Thousand Oaks, CA: Corwin.

Purkey, W. W., & Novak, J. M. (1996). *Inviting school success* (3rd ed.). Belmont, CA: Wadsworth.

Purkey, W. W., & Powell, D. (2005, Spring). An invitational approach to overcoming tough challenges in education. *Tennessee Principal, 25*–28.

Purkey, W. W., & Schmidt, J. J. (1996). *Invitational counseling.* Pacific Grove, CA: Brooks/Cole.

Ratledge, J. A. (2008, March). Hostage! *FORUM, 28*(2), 12–16. (Publication of the International Alliance for Invitational Education)

Rogers, C. R. (1951). *Client-centered therapy.* Boston: Houghton Mifflin.

Rogers, C. R. (1980). *A way of being.* Boston: Houghton Mifflin.

Schaub, A. R. (1991). The power of poor communications. *Journal of Educational Public Relations, 14*(3), 16–17.

Scheier, M. F., & Carver, C. S. (1993). On the power of positive thinking: The benefits of being optimistic. *Current Directions in Psychological Science, 1,* 26–30.

Schmidt, J. J. (2002). *Intentional helping: A philosophy for proficient caring relationships.* Upper Saddle River, NJ: Merrill/Prentice Hall.

Schmidt, J. J. (2004). *A survival guide for the elementary/middle school counselor.* San Francisco: Jossey-Bass.

Schmidt, J. J. (2008). *Counseling in schools: Comprehensive programs of responsive services for all students.* Boston: Allyn & Bacon.

Schmidt, J. J., & Medl, W. A. (1983). The six magic steps of consulting. *The School Counselor, 30,* 212–215.

Seligman, M. E. (1975). *Helplessness: On depression and death.* San Francisco: Freeman Press.

Seligman, M. E. (2006). *Learned optimism: How to change your mind and your life.* New York: Vintage.

Simons, T. (2008). *The integrity dividend: Leading by the poser of your word.* New York: Jossey-Bass.

Skiba, R., & Peterson, R. (1999). The dark side of zero tolerance: Can punishment lead to safe schools? *Phi Delta Kappan, 80*(5), 375–382.

Sweeney, T. J. (1998). *Adlerian counseling: A practitioner's approach* (4th ed.). Philadelphia: Accelerated Development.

Ury, W. (2008). *The power of positive no.* New York: Bantam.

Ury, W. L. (1993). *Getting past no: Negotiating with difficult people.* New York: Bantam Books.

Index

CORWIN
A SAGE Company

The Corwin logo—a raven striding across an open book—represents the union of courage and learning. Corwin is committed to improving education for all learners by publishing books and other professional development resources for those serving the field of PreK–12 education. By providing practical, hands-on materials, Corwin continues to carry out the promise of its motto: **"Helping Educators Do Their Work Better."**